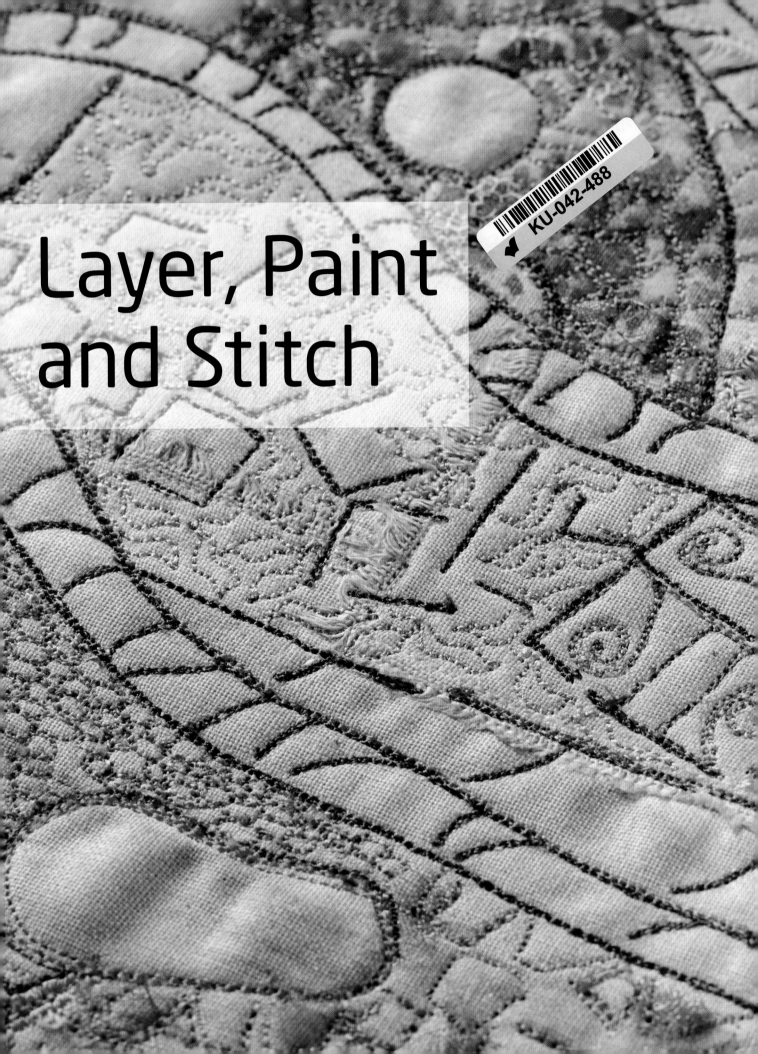

Layer, Paint and Stitch

DEDICATION
This book is dedicated to my mum,
who encouraged me to develop my
love of textiles.

With best wishes

Wendy Dolan

Layer, Paint and Stitch

CREATE TEXTILE ART USING FREEHAND MACHINE EMBROIDERY AND HAND STITCHING

WENDY DOLAN

SEARCH PRESS

ACKNOWLEDGEMENTS

My grateful thanks go to my supportive family and friends;
to my husband Rob, who has encouraged and supported
me throughout, and to my children, Kerry and Paul.
I would like to thank my sister, Julie Evans, who has helped
tirelessly proofreading my draft text and who knows the
content off by heart. For my wonderful students who
approach every class with enthusiasm and who have
waited patiently for this book to become a reality.

I would like to thank Roz Dace for approaching me
about the project, my editor Becky Shackleton for her
endless support and encouragement, and Paul Bricknell
for his excellent photography.

First published in 2015

Search Press Limited
Wellwood, North Farm Road,
Tunbridge Wells, Kent TN2 3DR

Illustrations and text copyright © Wendy Dolan, 2015

Photographs by Paul Bricknell at Search Press Studios

Photographs and design copyright © Search Press Ltd. 2015

ISBN: 978-1-78221-074-0

The Publishers and author can accept no responsibility for any
consequences arising from the information, advice or instructions
given in this publication.

Suppliers
If you have difficulty in obtaining any of the materials and equipment
mentioned in this book, then please visit the Search Press website for
details of suppliers: www.searchpress.com

You are invited to visit the author's website:
www.wendydolan.co.uk

Printed in China

Contents

Introduction

There is nothing more satisfying than creating something for yourself. I hope you will use this book as a journey of discovery in which my aim is to encourage you to experiment with techniques and to enjoy exploring their potential. You will see how to use a basic domestic sewing machine for freehand stitching, learning to 'draw' with thread to create exciting patterns, images and textures. The sewing machine is a wonderful tool and by practising simple exercises you can learn how to use it to create unique designs. It is rather like learning to drive – the more time you spend behind the wheel the more competent you become.

I love the tactile quality of fabric and thread and in this book I will show you how to piece and layer different weights of natural fabrics, such as calico, cotton, silk, linen, muslin, scrim and lace to create exciting surfaces. You will then see how to enhance the textural quality by developing both hand and machine stitching and experimenting with three-dimensional mediums and products. You will learn how to create tonal variations by applying paint to your layered and stitched background with brushes, palette knives, rollers and sponges, as each produces different effects. The fabrics will accept the paint in differing degrees and you have the freedom to blend colours. The projects that follow will build your confidence so that you can design and create your own individual artwork.

Once you are confident with your new skills, these different techniques can be combined to create three-dimensional objects such as cushion covers, book covers and vessels. You may also wish to use some techniques to decorate garments. I enjoy designing and embellishing bridal wear and have embroidered dress bodice panels, waistcoats, ties and dress trains. I designed and embroidered the lace adornment for my daughter's wedding dress, working on fine tulle netting, stabilised with soluble fabric and then freehand machine stitched. The embroidered lace was stitched in place over the main dress with pearls added by hand. Use this final section of the book as inspiration, to encourage you to develop your skills further.

My own journey, and enthusiasm for creating with fabric and thread, started early on when I was introduced to a variety of hand-embroidery techniques. Combined with my love of drawing and painting, I soon discovered that stitching, or mark-making with thread, allowed me to build exciting textured surfaces. During my degree course I discovered freehand machine embroidery and I continue to be amazed at the range of textures and original effects you can create on a basic sewing machine. Combining different stitching, painting and printing techniques gave me a broad range of skills with which to experiment and to help develop my own personal style; I hope you will develop your own approach to this fascinating medium. Inspiration comes from the world around me, the landscape, natural forms and architecture, so be open to what inspires you. In my recent series of work I explore the theme 'A Sense of Place', recording memorable places and journeys. Using maps as inspiration, landscapes and architectural images are interpreted with fabric, stitch and texture (see page 107).

There is no limit to the scale you can work on; you just have to plan carefully and work in sections. My commissions have included two embroidered stage curtains – 13 x 4.5m (42½ x 14¾ft) – for theatres on board the Royal Caribbean Cruise Liners *Legend of the Seas* and *Grandeur of the Seas*. These large artworks, *Starlight Serenade* and *Let's Dance*, combine screen-printed, painted, stitched and applied fabrics, with crystals, beads and sequins. *Aspiring Arches*, a wall-hung textile measuring 8.2 x 3.5m (27 x 11½ft), shown below, was commissioned by Ashridge Business School in Berkhamsted, Hertfordshire to celebrate the Millennium and depicted Ashridge's long history. I worked with my colleague Jae Maries over a period of four years to complete the work. Working on a large scale is challenging, however the design and working processes are very much the same as for smaller projects.

I hope the ideas in this book will inspire you and encourage you to develop skills that you can use in your own work. Above all have fun!

Aspiring Arches

Materials

There is an abundance of fabrics, paints and threads on the market and it can be quite overwhelming when you start to explore different techniques. I like to work with simple materials and this book will show you how to create wonderful effects without having to invest in expensive equipment and materials. It is always worth looking around charity shops and car-boot sales where you can often pick up unusual fabrics, threads and lace.

Fabrics

Any fabric can be used in a creative way. As you use this book, you will learn to consider the weight, fibre content and texture according to the purpose of your design. I like to work with plain, natural fabrics as they take all paints well and are a renewable resource. Try to build up a selection of fabrics with interesting textures so that you can select what is appropriate for any given task. Synthetic fabrics and sheers of various types can also be used to great effect.

Natural fibres

I prefer to use natural scoured cotton or pre-shrunk calico as my main base fabric as these have been commercially prepared ready to accept painting or printing directly. All other fabrics should be washed before use so that they do not shrink at a later stage. For practising stitch techniques, however, any firm cotton will be fine. Other natural fabrics that are good to experiment with are cottons, silk, silk noil, linen, cotton bump and batting, scrim, muslin, and cotton crepe bandages.

Synthetic fibres

Fabrics containing synthetic fibres, such as polyester, nylon, acetate, Kunin felt, velvet or satin also have their place. They can be used for dyeing and painting with disperse dyes and printing with transfer paints, crayons and inks.

Sheers

Sheer fabrics are semi-transparent and, when applied in layers, form attractive tonal variations. They can be distressed to create soft edges and manipulated to build raised surfaces. Organza, chiffon and voile are available in a wide range of colours, some of which are two-tone shot colours. I like to use very sheer nylon chiffon scarves to give a hint of colour to a design or to layer and then distress with a hot-air tool. Soldering irons can be used to burn away layers, creating amazing effects. Fine tulle netting is ideal for stitching lace.

Stabilisers

It is essential to place a stabiliser behind your work when you are machine stitching on woven fabric without an embroidery hoop. This will prevent your work from puckering. I use a medium-weight tearaway stabiliser, such as Stitch-n-Tear, but a heavy-weight interfacing such as Pelmet Vilene would also be acceptable. If you are embroidering on stretch-knit fabrics, such as jersey or Lycra, use a tearaway product so that you can remove the excess. Water-soluble stabilisers should be used for sheer or lightweight fabrics so that they can be washed away after stitching. A stabiliser can also be used to transfer designs from the reverse. This technique will be used in some of the projects.

Lace

Lace fabrics and trimmings and broderie anglaise come in a variety of patterns and add a beautiful surface texture. I look for designs that remind me of architectural carvings, and which will enhance my designs. Vintage lace can sometimes be found in charity shops and boot sales.

Non-woven synthetics

There is a wide range of non-woven products that can be used in creative stitching. Heavy-weight interfacings are ideal for making book covers and three-dimensional structures. Evolon is a white microfibre cloth that has a lovely suede-like feel. Lutradur is a unique bonded fabric that will react to heat, forming holes and exciting textures, as will Tyvek, a synthetic material that will bubble and shrink. All of these products can be coloured with fabric paints or transfer paints and inks.

Paints, dyes and 3D products

It can be quite daunting deciding which colouring products to work with. I mostly use a textile screen-printing pigment due to its versatility. It has a thick consistency so that it doesn't bleed onto the fabric, which makes it suitable for a variety of other applications – block printing, stencilling, monoprinting and painting. I sometimes use Procion dyes which are fibre-reactive dyes for natural fabrics. They come in powder form and are ideal for the cold water dyeing of fabrics and yarns. To add interest to your work you can use three-dimensional products such as Xpandaprint or puff paint, matt paint flakes and horticultural fleece to build up textures.

Paints and inks

There are many different paints and inks that can be used for design and to colour fabrics. Experiment in your sketchbook with acrylic, watercolour, water-soluble pencils and crayons, inks, marker pens, charcoal and pencils. It is less daunting if the pages have some colour on them before experimenting and drawing. Try using tea and coffee on paper and fabric to give lovely aged parchment effects.

Any of these products can be used to experiment on fabric, but most of them will not be permanent and therefore not suitable for garments or anything requiring washing, or for pictures that may need to be damp-stretched before mounting. Instead, choose pigments designed for fabric use – you should look for water-based products that are fixed with heat. Most will leave the fabric soft once dry – although some opaque products may leave a stiffer finish – and once ironed the colour will be permanent. There is a wide range of fabric paints available and they have different qualities: translucent, opaque, fluorescent, metallic and pearlescent. Silk paints can be used on any fabric and have intense colours, but like some other paints they are thin and therefore not suitable on their own for block printing, stencilling and monoprinting, or for controlling the flow when painted with a brush. They can, however, be mixed with powder-based thickening agents that can convert them into a paste for direct painting. Procion fibre-reactive dyes can also be thickened in this way. Colours can be mixed before applying to the fabric, offering a range of shades and tones.

Water-based fabric screen-printing inks are very versatile and are my preferred choice. They are thick and therefore suitable for all methods of application. The bright, vivid colours can be mixed on a palette and, using an extender base, they can be lightened without altering the consistency. They can also be diluted with water and applied with a brush, giving interesting colour-wash effects; the fabric is then left soft to handle. A water spray can be used to dampen the fabric before applying the paint and this can give some beautiful results. Select what suits you by experimenting with different products.

Transfer paints, dyes and crayons

Some colouring products are available that can be worked on paper and then transferred onto fabric. Transfer paints and inks can be applied onto computer paper with a brush or stamped with printing blocks to produce different patterns and effects. Transfer crayons can be used to take paper rubbings from textured surfaces and then overlaid with transfer paint. When the paper is dry it can be placed, coloured side down, onto fabric and ironed to transfer the colour to the fabric. You will need to protect the iron and ironing board with non-stick baking parchment. Several prints can be made and you can try overprinting. For best results these products should be transferred onto synthetic fabrics.

Three-dimensional fabric media

Three-dimensional fabric media such as Xpandaprint or puff paint are acid-free products that can be used on paper or textiles. When heated with a hot-air tool or iron they expand to produce a raised surface, giving fascinating sculptural and textural effects. They come in paste form that can be applied with a sponge, palette knife, brush or through a stencil and can be painted after heating. The textures created are great for interpreting moss, lichen, coral, rust and crumbling stonework and can easily be stitched into.

Horticultural fleece

Horticultural fleece is a thin, non-woven fabric that is used to protect plants from frost and can be purchased from garden centres. It is a wonderful addition to your fabric collection as it melts with heat and can be ironed or zapped with a hot-air tool to create heightened textures.

Matt paint flakes

These resemble real bits of peeling paint and can be used to construct wonderful distressed images. They are available in a range of natural architectural shades and can be coloured over the top. They are adhered to the surface with either glue or paint, but as the results are not washable they are most suitable for decorative effects.

General equipment

You do not have to buy expensive equipment in order to experiment in your design work. Most of the items used in this book can be purchased in art shops or on the internet and you will soon discover that you can produce pleasing effects by experimenting with a range of brushes, palette knives, rollers and sponges, both on paper and fabric.

Brushes

A range of brushes can be used, depending on the purpose. Wide brushes are appropriate for covering large areas of fabric whereas fine ones can be used for small details. Short stubby bristles are good for working paint into textured surfaces. Sponge brushes can give different effects, and an old toothbrush or nailbrush can be used for splatter painting.

Palette knives

Palette knives, or painting knives, are good for mixing and applying paint to fabric and scraping three-dimensional fabric products such as Xpandaprint or puff paint through stencils. They come in a variety of sizes and should be quite flexible. As a substitute you can try using an old credit card.

Sponges and rollers

Sponges are used to apply paint through stencils and onto printing blocks. They can also create attractive textures when sponged directly onto fabric. Natural sponges are best as they have a variety of structures to their surface. Three-dimensional fabric products such as Xpandaprint or puff paint can be applied with a sponge but you must rinse it after use or they will harden on the sponge.

Masking tape

A low-tack masking tape is useful for holding designs in place while drawing or tracing. I also recommend it is used to mask and protect areas of fabric when you are painting and to hold stencils in position.

Non-stick baking parchment

Non-stick baking parchment can be purchased in any supermarket and is essential when working with heat-reactive products. Teflon baking sheets can also be used.

Transfer adhesive

Iron-on transfer adhesive is a paper-backed adhesive film that can be used to apply one fabric to another by ironing. It can also be painted and used in many creative ways. Always make sure you protect the iron and ironing board with non-stick baking parchment and wait for it to cool down before removing the paper.

Glue

I choose not to use glue when I am working with fabrics but I do use a glue stick and PVA glue in my sketchbook.

Stencils

You can cut and make your own stencils from plain newsprint or similar paper and then apply paint through them with a sponge or stencil brush. When dry they can be ironed and re-used. Paper doilies, lace, rug canvas and sequin waste can also produce lovely effects. Acetate sheets can be cut with a soldering iron to produce a more permanent stencil. There are, however, a wide range of commercially produced stencils that you might like to use. I find the ones with textural effects most useful, or those that resemble carvings or architectural details.

Wooden printing blocks

A wide range of wooden printing blocks are available to purchase or you could make your own. For example, you can cut out shapes from sheets of self-adhesive foam and stick them onto a piece of wood or foam core board, or use matchsticks or string arranged in a pattern and stuck onto a block of wood. Apply paint or printing medium with a sponge or roller and then press down onto your fabric. All sorts of everyday objects can be used for block printing: bubble wrap, foam, cotton reels, edges of card, and even leaves.

Hot-air tool and soldering iron

A hot-air tool or heat gun is a useful addition to your workbox. It can be used with products such as Xpandaprint or puff paint, horticultural fleece, Lutradur and Tyvek. It can also be used to distress synthetic fabrics like chiffon and organza. A 350 watt gun is ideal. A hair dryer is useful for drying painted fabric but is not hot enough to take the place of a heat gun. A soldering iron is another wonderful tool. It can be used to burn away layers of synthetic fabric and to fuse fabrics together. It can also be used to cut out shapes from non-woven products such as heavy-weight interfacing and Evolon and for making stencils from acetate sheets. A rest should always be used and you can work on a piece of glass or an old chopping board.

TAKE CARE

Great care should be taken when working with heat tools.

Always work in a well-ventilated room. Fumes may build up when working with some fibres so you may wish to wear a mask or respirator, especially if you are pregnant or suffer from breathing difficulties.

Work on a stable, heatproof surface. An ironing board, ironing pad, or baking parchment on a towel are ideal.

Sewing equipment

The sewing equipment you need to try out the ideas in this book is quite simple. The only expensive item is a sewing machine. If you do not have access to a machine then there are lots of ideas you can try out with hand stitching. A basic sewing kit and a few threads is all you need to get started.

Sewing machine

Any basic domestic sewing machine can be used for freehand machine embroidery. All you need is straight stitch and zigzag and to be able to lower or cover the teeth or feed dogs. It is extremely useful if you have an extension table for your machine. This helps to support an embroidery hoop if you are using one, and your work in general. It is well worth investing in some extra bobbins as you will want to work with different colours when you start experimenting with your stitching. I will be showing you how to adjust the tensions on your machine to build some textural stitch effects and at that stage you may find it useful to buy a spare bobbin case. Always buy bobbins and accessories that are specific to your model of machine or you may seriously damage the hook and race mechanism.

Darning and freehand embroidery feet

You can buy a darning foot or freehand embroidery foot to fit any machine – some are specific to a particular make and others are universal. It replaces the standard sewing foot and has a spring that allows you the freedom to stitch in any direction. The darning foot raises and lowers with the machine needle as you stitch, stabilising the fabric to ensure a good stitch. An open-toe darning foot will give you greater visibility when stitching. A freehand quilting foot is available for some machines and is useful for stitching across thicker layers of fabric as there is a bit more space under the foot.

Scissors

Curved or double curved tip scissors, often called duck-billed or appliqué scissors, allow easy close cutting of threads without the risk of damaging fabrics. But any small, sharp embroidery scissors or snips will be suitable. A larger pair of dressmaking scissors will be needed for cutting fabrics.

Embroidery hoop

I would recommend a good-quality wooden embroidery hoop with a strong brass bracket and a screw that can be tightened with a screwdriver. You will find it worthwhile binding the inner ring of your hoop with a narrow cotton tape. This helps to maintain the tension and to protect your fabric. An 18 or 20cm (7 or 8in) hoop is practical but you may find it useful to have a few different sizes.

Miscellaneous

These are useful items to have in your workbox:

• Tweezers to position small pieces of fabric and remove any loose threads from your machine.

• A wooden skewer to hold fabrics or thread in position near your needle while you are sewing – much better than using your fingers!

• A kilt pin to help to guide temperamental threads through your machine.

Needles and pins

Use good-quality needles for your machine. The higher the number, the larger the needle, so make sure you are using the appropriate size. This is relevant to the weight of thread you are using and the thickness of fabric you are stitching into. I usually work with a 90/14 or a 100/16, unless I am stitching on finer fabrics; for these I would use an 80/12 or 70/10. Top-stitch needles have larger eyes and are extra strong. Machine needles have a protective groove down the front edge and your thread tucks inside this channel every time the needle makes a stitch. If you are using too fine a needle your thread will be proud of the groove and rub against the fabric as you stitch. This can cause the thread to shred.

For hand stitching it is useful to have a range of embroidery and crewel needles. Chenille needles have large elongated eyes and sharp points and are suitable for different thicknesses of yarn.

I like to use glass-headed pins when I work; flowerhead pins used by quilters are also worth trying.

Threads

Any machine thread can be used for freehand machine embroidery. Polyester and cotton threads are perfect for practising and will have a matt finish. In the projects you will begin by working with a white or cream cotton or silk thread while stitching down layers of fabric. However, when you begin to stitch into your designs there are some wonderful machine-embroidery threads on the market that offer a striking range of colours and finishes. Rayon threads have a beautiful lustre and are available in a range of strong vibrant colours, plain, shaded and variegated. Metallic threads can give a rich shimmer and sparkle.

For hand stitching I like to vary the weight and finish of the threads and yarns I use to create rich textures. Cotton perlé, coton à broder, stranded cotton, crochet cotton, fine wool, linen and machine threads can all generate eye-catching effects. The more textural variety, the better.

Inspiration

How do our surroundings inspire our creative artwork? I am always being asked 'Where do you get your ideas from?' The answer is 'Everywhere'. Wherever we look we can find inspiration. Our ever-changing surroundings are affected by the seasons, climatic conditions, construction and decay. The important thing is to keep observing and recording what you see. You can then work with your ideas and experiment. I am always encouraging my students to keep a notebook or sketchbook with them so they can make drawings, quick sketches and notes about things that catch their eye or inspire them. Taking photographs is an ideal way of recording your observations as you can then develop your ideas later on.

Where to start

The world's landscapes provide a constant source of inspiration, from rolling hills to open plains and craggy mountains, and from rippling brooks to raging rivers and cascading waterfalls. Aerial views allow you to study the patchwork of field patterns and meandering river courses, while the coast exposes a myriad of contrasts from sand dunes and cliffs to waves and rock pools. Closer studies reveal the many exciting textures found within those environments: rocks and strata can be studied for their line, form, structure and texture, as well as the wonderful colours found in their layers. Trees and tree bark provide fascinating forms, shapes and textures, whether you are looking at individual trees, a copse or a forest. The forest floor reveals snowdrops, wood anemones and bluebells in the spring and a textured blanket of brightly coloured leaves in the autumn, hiding toadstools and fungi. The seasons present a constantly changing vista from the bare branches of winter, to the fresh green shoots of spring, the rich foliage of summer and the glowing colours of autumn.

Flowers can offer many starting points for design. Natural, wild flowers in meadows or hedgerows show the beauty of our native plants, while gardens often display a wonderful array of colour in herbaceous borders and in containers and pots. Detailed studies can uncover the patterns and veins of delicate petals and stamens, seed heads and foliage.

I also love looking at the surfaces and textures of walls: dry-stone walls covered in moss or lichen, flint walls, or brick and plaster walls that have become weathered and distressed. In other architecture around us we can study the shape and structure of buildings and the details such as windows and doors, arches, tiles, mosaics, balconies and rusting ironwork and peeling paintwork.

When I am on holiday, or travelling, I am always inspired by the variety within different cultures, the wonderful colours and patterns in the textiles and costumes, the architectural wonders and the landscapes. Egypt, Venice, France and Barcelona have all featured in my work. If you are unable to visit other countries, museums are well worth a visit and provide a wealth of objects to be enjoyed and studied.

Looking at the work of other artists can widen your experience and prompt you to question what you like, to consider composition and the use of colour. Amongst others, I particularly admire the art of Antoni Gaudi, Gustav Klimt, Dale Chihuly the glass sculptor, Wassily Kandinsky and Paul Klee. John Piper, an English painter, graphic artist and designer, is very influential in my own work. He was particularly noted for his paintings of architectural views, especially of churches and stately homes. His pen work produces details of his subject over a background painted with strong, bold colours. I am inspired to use freehand machine stitching over textured and painted fabrics.

I hope you will find your own inspiration from 'everywhere'!

Colour

The choice of colour in your design work will have an immediate impact on the viewer. It is a strong element that affects our moods and emotions and creates atmosphere – it should be carefully considered. I encourage my students to spend time collecting coloured papers and fabrics and to practise mixing paint colours. This might be acrylics and watercolours that they are using in their sketchbooks, or fabric paints for use on cloth.

The colour wheel

An artist's colour wheel is a useful tool to help you understand how colours relate to each other and how to mix them to create a wider variety. The three primary colours, or hues, are red, blue and yellow and all other colours on the wheel are mixed from these. By combining any two of these colours you will produce the secondary colours: violet, green and orange. A third set of colours, the tertiary colours, fill in the six gaps between the primary and secondary colours: red-orange, blue-green, red-violet and so on. Colours on the opposite side of the colour wheel are complementary and will produce a muddy brown if mixed together. As you experiment with mixing colours you will soon learn the variations created by adjusting the proportions. To make the colours paler and less concentrated add white paint, extender base, or water if using water-based pigment. These are referred to as tints. Tones are created by adding grey, and this softens the intensity of the colours. You will also want to create shades – this is achieved by adding black. However, some black pigments should be used sparingly as they can change the character of the colours quite dramatically. As you plan your piece try to consider the colours that work well together to create a balanced and pleasing result.

The colour wheel shows the relationship between the primary, secondary and tertiary colours. It is a useful tool to help you choose colour schemes for your work.

Colour schemes

Complementary

For this colour scheme choose colours that are opposite each other on the wheel, red and green, or yellow and violet, for example. These opposing colours will create maximum contrast so it works best if one is dominant and the other is used as an accent.

Monochromatic

A monochromatic colour scheme uses shades, tints and tones of just one colour.

Analogous

Analogous colour schemes use colours that are next to each other on the colour wheel. Often found in nature, analogous colour schemes usually match well and are harmonious and easy on the eye.

Triadic

A triadic colour scheme uses three colours that are evenly spaced around the colour wheel, forming a triangle. This works well if one of the colours is dominant and the other two are used for contrasting accents. Try mixing the three colours together to give some interesting hues.

Selecting a colour scheme

Colour schemes can be informed by the world around us and I find that nature is one of the best sources of inspiration. Complementary colours are seen with red poppies in a green field, yellow beards on a purple iris; analogous colours emerge in autumn leaves or on a frosty morning. Many great designers and artists derive their inspiration from the natural world and this can give us many ideas to work with. Be adventurous when you are exploring colour schemes though and don't feel you have to work to a formula. These are guides to help you get started and to encourage you to discover what works for you. Remember, flowers don't have to be pink and leaves don't have to be green, so choose unpredictable colours and have fun experimenting.

Warm and cool colour combinations

Colours are considered to be warm or cool. Generally, warm colours are those in the red, orange and yellow sector of the colour wheel, while cool ones are in the green, blue and violet sector. Warm colours tend to be quite strong and dramatic and appear to advance towards the viewer while cool colours have a calm, tranquil effect, with a tendency to recede towards the background. Awareness of these aspects can help create space, balance and depth in your work.

Painting fabrics

A good way to explore working with colour is to mix a range of coloured paints and then select an assortment of plain fabrics. Start to apply the colour and just see what happens. The diverse fibres will each absorb the paint differently. You could apply the paints with a brush, sponge or palette knife using any of the techniques suggested on the following pages. By building up a collection of fabrics, using the rainbow of colours in the colour wheel, you will be able to use them as samples when choosing colour schemes.

Using coloured threads

Try to build up a selection of threads for both machine and hand stitching. You can then experiment to see what colour effects are produced by various thread combinations and by stitching into different coloured fabrics. By working with two threads in the needle on the machine (see page 24) or by hand, you can keep changing the colours of thread to build up rich background textures. Start with four different shades of blue thread, then change the combination of colours in your needle. You could retain the dark thread but keep changing the other shades. Then see what happens when you use complementary thread colours.

Photo-editing software

If you have photo-editing programs on your computer you can experiment with colour variations by altering the hue and saturation levels of your photographs, creating some exciting combinations – see below.

Freehand machine stitching

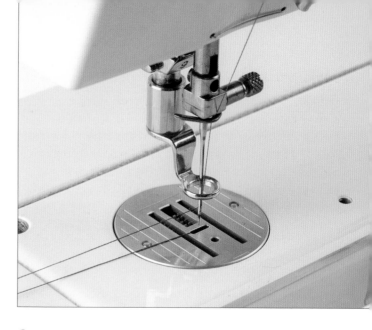

Prepare your machine

1 Lower the teeth or feed dogs or, on some machines, cover them with a metal or plastic darning plate. Do check your machine manual if you are not sure where to locate this facility. If you have misplaced your darning plate you can cover the feed dogs with a piece of masking tape, making a hole for the needle. Set the stitch length to zero. From now on you will be in control of the length and direction of the stitching.

2 Remove the presser foot, including the short shank if your machine uses clip-on feet. This can be replaced with a darning foot or freehand embroidery foot which raises and lowers with the needle, stabilising the fabric while you are stitching but allowing you the freedom to move in any direction. If you can get the fabric tight enough in an embroidery hoop you can stitch without a foot at all. This gives you greater visibility but do keep your hands well away from the needle!

Prepare the fabric in a hoop

When you start experimenting with freehand machine stitching it is a good idea to work with an embroidery hoop.

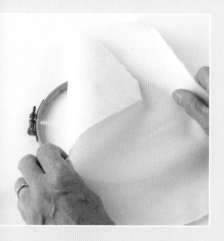

1 Place the outer ring of your hoop (the part with the screw) on a table. Lay your fabric on top.

2 Position the inner ring on top of the fabric and push into position. Pull the fabric until it is drum tight, then use a screwdriver to tighten the hoop's screw.

Prepare your fabric with tearaway stabiliser

It is not always practical to work in an embroidery hoop as you might be working with several layers of fabric and it may leave a mark on some fabrics. If you are working on a large design it can also be quite inconvenient to keep moving the hoop around from one area to another. Without the support of a hoop you should stabilise the cloth to prevent it from puckering. Pin a piece of tearaway stabiliser in place underneath your fabric.

You are now ready to stitch. Place your fabric under the needle. If you have difficulty positioning your hoop under the darning foot you will find that your presser-foot lever will lift up a bit further, allowing easier access.

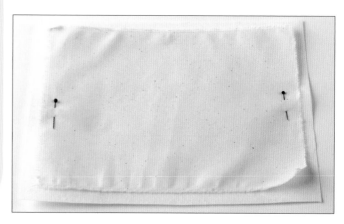

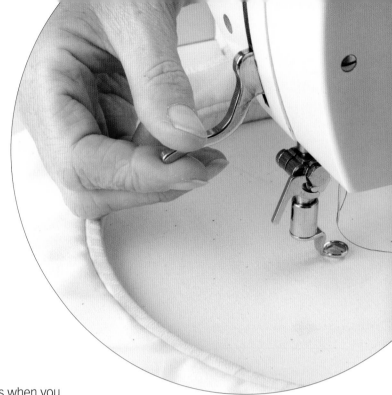

Lower the presser–foot lever

One of the most important parts of your machine is the presser-foot lever. Not only does it raise and lower the foot on your machine, it also engages the top thread tension. You must lower the presser-foot lever when you are ready to stitch. Use the 'tug test' by pulling your top thread to make sure it has tension on it. If you do forget to lower the lever you will end up with a knotted 'birds' nest' on the underside of your work!

Bring up the bobbin thread

It is important to be in control of both top and bottom threads when you start to stitch otherwise they can become tangled underneath. This can be prevented by bringing the bobbin thread up onto the surface of the fabric.

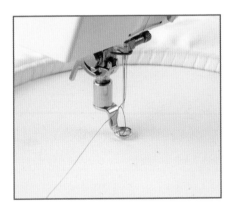
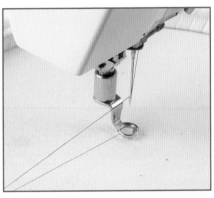
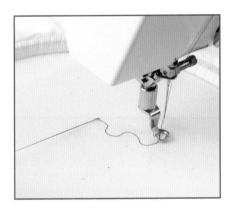

1 Hold onto the top thread with your left hand and give it the 'tug test' to check you have lowered the presser-foot lever. Turn the handwheel towards you, taking the needle in and out of the fabric until the take-up lever is in its highest position. Pull the needle thread and the bobbin thread will come up through the fabric. If your machine is electronic you may have a button which you can use to lower and raise the needle, or you may be able to tap the foot pedal once. Use this facility to bring up the bobbin thread.

2 Pull the loop through and hold onto both threads at the side of your hoop.

3 Think of your hoop like a clock face and position your hands at a 'quarter to three', on the left and right. Run the machine at a medium to fast speed and move the frame steadily. You are free to stitch in any direction so start to draw and doodle with your thread. Try to relax and breathe!

> ## TIPS
>
> *Keep your feet under your chair and only move your foot onto the foot pedal when the machine is prepared and your hands are clear of the needle.*
>
> *Keep your hands well away from the needle when you are stitching.*

Machining tips

With practise you will soon be creating patterns and textures with ease. Take time to experiment with different threads and fabrics and you will gradually learn more about your machine. The processes will become more natural and instinctive. There are various tips that I suggest to my students to make life easier and I hope you will find some of them useful.

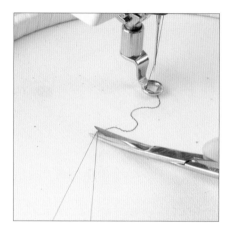

Trimming threads

Make a few stitches on the spot when you start and finish. This secures the threads so that they won't unravel. Using a pair of small curved scissors allows you to trim the threads close to the fabric with ease. However, you may wish to take threads through to the back of the piece and tie off, if you are working on a garment.

Moving from one area to another

When you wish to move from one area of your fabric to another you must remember to raise the presser-foot lever to release the top-thread tension. When you get to where you want to continue you must remember to lower the lever again. You can trim the joining threads when you are finished.

Using a skewer

A wooden skewer is an ideal tool to use when you are working, and you can use it in a few different ways. You can hold down loose or small scraps of fabric while applying them to your designs – which is much better than using your fingers! You can also use one to help pull through the bobbin thread when you start to stitch.

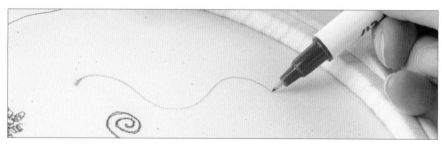

Taking a line for a walk

An excellent exercise to help you develop control of your machine is to draw a line on your fabric and then try to stitch over it. Water- and air-soluble fabric markers can be used to mark guidelines. They can be erased with water or will simply fade over time, but do take care and always test them out on your material first to make sure they don't leave a watermark.

Allowing the thread to run smoothly

All machines are different and some threads run more easily than others. Some shiny and metallic threads can unravel and catch round the spool pin but there are ways to help you stop this from happening. You might want to start by loosening the top tension, as this can help, but all these suggestions can help to stop thread slipping and unravelling.

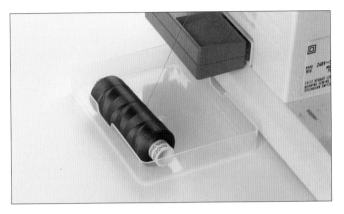

Threads can be put in a small box or jam jar and placed behind the machine. They can then be hooked round the spool pin or through a kilt pin as far right, for cones.

Large cones of thread will not fit on top of your machine. They can, however, stand on the table behind and either hook round one of your spool pins or you can attach a kilt pin to the back of the machine with masking tape and pass the thread through the hole at the end. You could also wind cone thread onto a spare bobbin and use it on top of the machine, weighting it down with an empty cotton reel.

Attach a kilt pin to your spare spool holder so the thread can be lifted as it leaves the reel. Some machines have a hole in the top of the second spool pin through which the thread can pass or there may be a wire hook at the back of the carrying handle. A cop of thread can be placed on a small circular pad of foam to stop the thread sliding down.

Top threads breaking

It can be very annoying if your top thread keeps breaking. Try loosening the top-thread tension and increase your needle size, or use a top-stitch needle with a larger eye.

Extension table

It is really useful to have an extension table for your machine to support your work. Alternatively, you may find that placing a pile of books or a large block of polystyrene (the same height as your machine bed) alongside will help. Some machines slope down at the front so the aim is to try to keep your embroidery hoop as level as possible.

Thread tensions

Do not worry too much if your threads seem to be pulling up small loops from underneath. It may be that you are using different weights of thread but the results can add texture and interest. You will gradually learn how to adjust your machine tensions and correct this effect if you wish.

Masking tape on the feed dogs

If your machine requires a darning plate to cover the feed dogs you may find it easier to fix a piece of masking tape over the teeth instead. Make a hole for the needle and set the stitch length to zero so that the tape doesn't tear. This can be less bulky and gives more room for your hoop.

Straight stitch

Most of my freehand stitching is created using a basic straight stitch. Once you have lowered the feed dogs and attached a darning foot to your machine you are in control of moving the fabric. You can now start creating different effects as you determine both the direction and length of the stitch depending on the speed at which you move the fabric and how fast you run the machine. A fast machine speed but slow movement of the fabric will create a short stitch length. Slowing down the machine and moving the fabric more quickly will produce a longer stitch length, creating attractive variations.

Your stitch direction can be used to interpret line, form, movement and texture so consider these design elements as you experiment. If your bobbin thread is showing as small loops on the surface, use it to good effect and choose your thread colours to show some contrast, or use the same colour in the top and bottom. Loosening the top tension will help to stop this from happening.

Start by making patterns and shapes as if you were doodling with a pencil: create zigzags and swirls, try cross-hatching, write your name and draw simple shapes such as flowers. Another good technique to try is to run the machine fast and move the fabric in very small circles. This is ideal for filling in and creating a crusty texture, and is known as granite stitch. Change your thread colour and see what happens when you repeat patterns on top of each other, building up layers.

Apply small pieces of coloured fabric to your background using transfer adhesive or by holding them in place with a skewer. Then start stitching across the design in all directions, shading areas with lines of straight stitch. Change colour and try working with a variegated thread. See what happens when you use layers of sheer fabric to create different tonal effects. Save any exciting pieces to be made up into small bags, purses or book covers.

You can achieve heavier effects if you work with two threads in your needle. Most machines have two spool pins to allow the use of two threads but, if not, you can place one in a jar or box on the table (see page 23) or wind one onto a bobbin, placing it on the spool pin with the reel of thread on top of it. You must loosen the top tension slightly and use a larger needle (100/16) to accommodate the thicker thread. Hold both strands together while threading and only separate them if you can see your tension disc, placing one either side of it so they are both held under tension. You may see some loops on the surface as the tension may not be totally even, but this can add to the composition. Use different combinations of plain and variegated colours, building up dense areas of stitch.

Zigzag stitch

If you have a swing needle your machine can also be used for freehand zigzag stitching, producing endless possibilities for creating patterns, textures and blending colours. Set your stitch selector to zigzag and the stitch length to zero (some electronic machines will only lower to 0.2). When starting and finishing, keep the width control set to zero to stop threads coming undone, then select a width setting and begin to experiment. You may need to loosen the top-thread tension slightly.

Try building up layers of stitch by using different colours. It will look like a zigzag if you move the fabric away from you or towards you but try moving the fabric from side to side and you will create horizontal lines of long stitches, which could be ideal to suggest water, clouds or pathways.

Shaky zigzag is great for tree foliage, cornfield stubble, forest floors and general backgrounds. Imagine you are using a garden sieve and want to sift the soil. You shake it backwards, forwards and sideways at the same time. That is how you should move your fabric to create this versatile effect. Experiment with different widths of stitch but ensure the machine is running fast as you shake the fabric in short sharp movements, otherwise you might break your needle.

Combine different coloured threads while you build up layers of zigzag and try stitching over fabric scraps. If your machine has a variable control you can alter the width of the zigzag as you are stitching but you will only have one hand to move the fabric and you must run the machine quite fast. The more you experiment, the more forms you will discover, until you have built up a collection of samples that you can refer to when working on future projects.

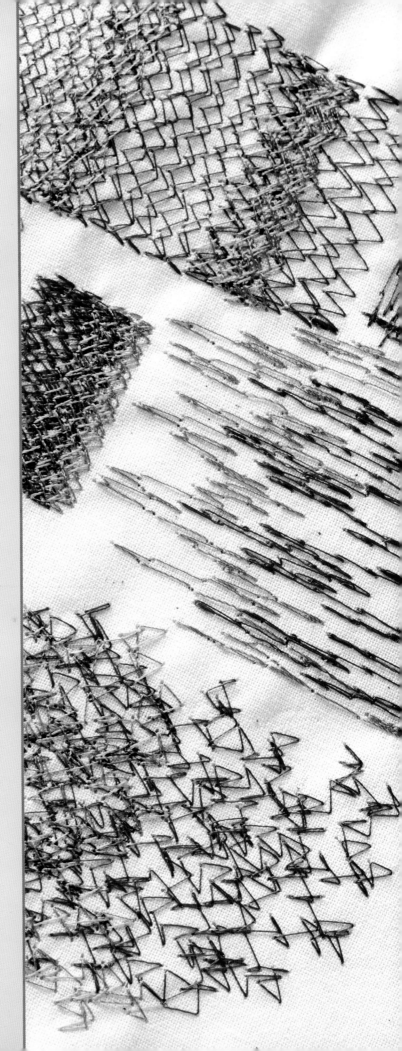

Satin stitch

Satin stitch is a variation of zigzag but you move the fabric at a constant steady speed, creating an even, short stitch length. With the width set at zero make a few stitches on the spot to secure the threads then select a width setting and run the machine fast, moving the fabric slowly and steadily. The stitch will become a more open zigzag if you suddenly move the fabric too quickly, so practise as much as you can. Vary the widths on your machine and build up rows of stitching so you can see what different effects you can achieve. If you want a perfectly smooth stitch it is usually best to loosen the top tension slightly as this can prevent the bobbin thread from showing on the edges. However, when the bobbin thread is visible it can produce intriguing forms so you could use it to your advantage, tightening the top tension to pull the bobbin thread up. Satin stitch can tend to pull the fabric so, if a looser tension does not help, you can place some tearaway stabiliser behind the work.

Try using a variety of threads when you are experimenting as you can get some exciting results. Machine-embroidery rayon threads have a beautiful sheen and satin stitch can really show them to their best advantage. Metallic threads can give a rich surface and random-dyed threads produce fascinating effects. Variegated and shaded threads can appear as blocks of colour, often revealing stripes.

Bolder lines can be created by stitching a wide row of satin stitch over a narrow one, giving a padded appearance. Or a similar effect can be achieved by satin stitching over a length of yarn or string that has been anchored with an open zigzag stitch first. This is ideal for outlining designs and giving definition.

Whip stitch

After experimenting with patterns and textures using straight, zigzag and satin stitch you can start to create remarkable effects by altering the tensions on your machine. You will still be working with the three basic stitches but achieving interesting raised textures. Whip stitch is a wonderful stitch. The top thread lies on the surface of the fabric and the bobbin thread is pulled up through the fabric in loops to cover, or 'whip' it.

In order to explore the versatility of whip stitch you need to adjust the tensions on your machine. The top thread tension is easily altered. Using a strong thread (polyester is ideal), gradually tighten the tension dial until the bobbin thread shows on the surface of your fabric when stitching. Invisible monofilament nylon thread is very strong and works beautifully for this technique, producing small dots of colour. A soft machine-embroidery rayon thread works best in the bobbin as it should pull through easily. However, this setting can be quite limited and you can only explore the full potential of this stitch if you also adjust the tension of your bobbin. Don't be afraid of adjusting your bobbin tensions! Just make sure you record any adjustments so you can easily return the tension to normal.

Adjusting your bobbin

Your machine may have a vertical removable bobbin case or a horizontal fixed bobbin case with a drop-in bobbin. You may have to remove the needle plate on your machine to access the screw. If you make a note of the normal (current) position of the tension screw you can then make adjustments according to the minutes on a clock using a small screwdriver. Start by making small changes, turning maybe fifteen or thirty minutes to the left, loosening the screw. Provided you record what you are doing you will be able to reverse the action and return the bobbin case back to its normal tension.

Now you can begin building exciting textural stitch effects. Try small adjustments at a time, running the machine at a medium to fast speed and moving your fabric slowly and carefully. The bobbin thread will come up to the surface, creating fascinating results. Vary the stitch length to form different textures and experiment with a variety of thread combinations. See what you can achieve when you work with zigzag and satin stitch as well as a straight stitch. If you use whip stitch a lot it might be worth investing in a spare bobbin case for your machine. Otherwise you will need to remember to return your tensions to normal after stitching.

REMEMBER

To loosen – turn anticlockwise to the left.
To tighten – turn clockwise to the right.

You may find it easier to remember 'lefty loosey'
and 'righty tighty'!

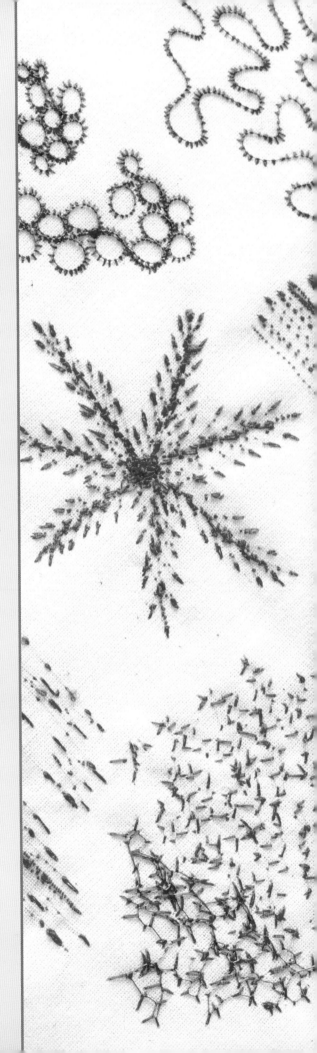

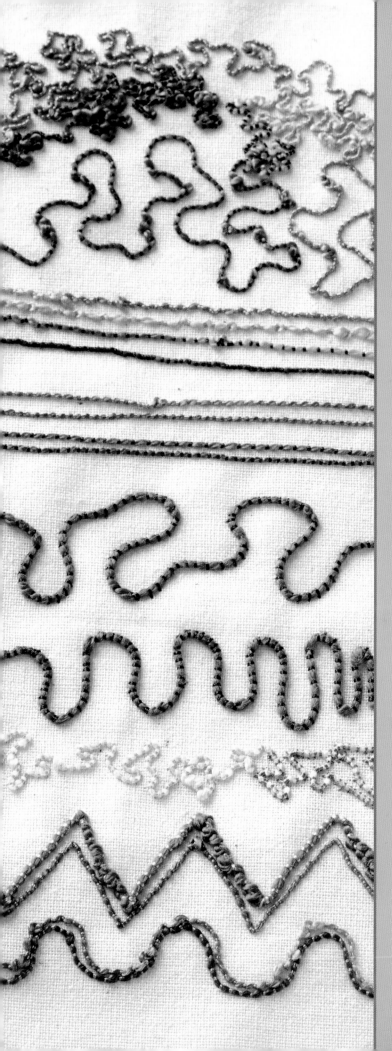

Cable stitch

Some threads and yarns are too thick to use on the top of the machine but they can be used in the bobbin. By loosening or removing the tension screw on your bobbin case (or by-passing the bobbin tension on drop-in bobbin machines) these thicker threads can create rich textures and can be wound by hand or machine onto the bobbin (see facing page). Carefully loosen or remove the bobbin's tension screw, making a note of any adjustments, and put the screw in a safe place if you remove it!

Cable stitch can produce an effect similar to couching (see page 30) and is ideal for outlining shapes with bold raised lines and for textures resembling moss, lichen and foliage. Stretch your fabric upside down in an embroidery hoop, or place stabilised fabric upside down, as you will be stitching from the wrong side with the thicker bobbin thread creating the design underneath. It is important to bring the bobbin thread up onto the surface before you start stitching. This can be made easier by lowering your needle into the fabric and moving the fabric around to open up a small hole, or by using a stiletto.

It can be a bit daunting as you can't see what you are actually sewing but with practise you will learn to judge how much texture is being created. Work steadily and try not to cross over your lines of stitching as it may become too thick underneath and the needle might break. Try altering the top tension to see what varied effects you can make. A looser top tension will produce a smooth couched line; a tighter top tension will create a more uneven, beaded effect. Change the stitch length too – with a short stitch length the top thread will almost completely cover the lower thread, giving a finish similar to whip stitch.

Experiment with a wide variety of yarns such as cotton perlé, crochet cotton, ribbon thread and wool. Chenille, bouclé and metallic knitting yarns can give a lovely texture. Try using a contrasting colour, or use variegated and metallic threads on the top of your machine. Once you have created some textures, turn your fabric over and start to stitch into your design on the right side with straight stitch, zigzag or satin stitch. You will soon find that you can develop a whole range of results and you can enjoy experimenting with this array of machine-stitch effects.

TIP
Wind several bobbins before you begin a project as each bobbin will not hold many metres of yarn.

Loading a bobbin with thicker thread

You can machine wind bobbins with thick thread. This helps to give an even wrap, resulting in smoother stitching. Make sure you cut the first end close to the bobbin so you don't leave any loose thread. Alternatively you can wrap by hand, keeping it as even as possible.

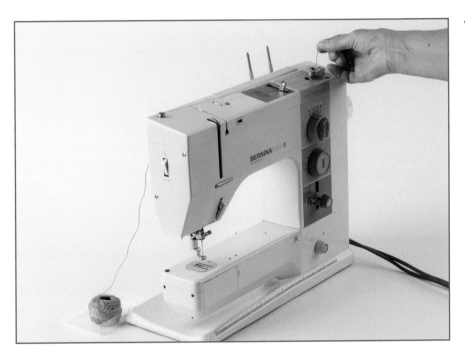

1 Find a suitable box, jar or cup and place the reel or cone inside, positioning it on the table behind your machine. Place the thread around the bobbin winding thread guide and then put it through a hole in the top of your bobbin on the winder spindle, holding it in your right hand. This will ensure a tight wrap when the bobbin starts to fill. Wind the bobbin, making sure the thread doesn't slip out of the thread guide on the top of your machine and then cut the beginning thread end as close as possible to the bobbin.

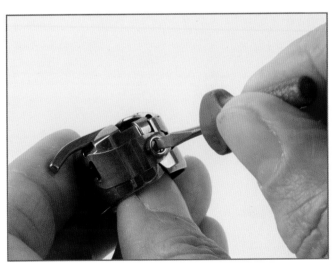

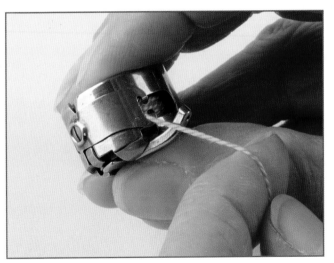

2 As you are running a thicker thread through your bobbin case you will need to loosen the tension screw to accommodate it (see page 27). For some thicker yarns you may need to remove the screw completely but make sure you put it somewhere safe! Experiment with different tensions.

3 Place the bobbin in the bobbin case, draw the thread through the slot and under the tension spring – or around the spring on a horizontal fixed bobbin case. The thread should now run smoothly or loosely, depending on the effects you wish to create. If your machine has a drop-in bobbin you have the option of bypassing the tension screw completely and just bringing the thread up through the needle plate. This will create the loosest tension possible.

Hand stitching

Hand stitching can create wonderful surface textures, lines and patterns. You can work with any number of stitches but I prefer to keep to a few simple ones and vary the effects by changing the type, weight and thickness of the threads used. Think of your stitching as mark making and drawing rather than trying to make a particular kind of stitch, and try working on different fabrics. Those which are not too closely woven can be easier to stitch into and, therefore, it is easier to build up rich surfaces. Using a suitable needle can also make the task simpler. A chenille needle has a large eye and a sharp point and will pass through your work with ease. You can choose whether to work in an embroidery hoop or not, but a hoop can help to keep the fabric taut and prevent it from puckering. Hand stitching can complement your freehand machine work, and vice versa, and you can have great fun exploring a wide range of materials and techniques.

Straight stitch

Straight stitch is the simplest and most versatile stitch. As the name implies, it is a straight line that can be worked in any direction and can be spaced at varying intervals. It can outline shapes and give shading. Curved lines can be created by working several straight stitches close together and overlapping them. This sample uses a selection of different weights and shades of thread and can be used to represent foliage and grasses.

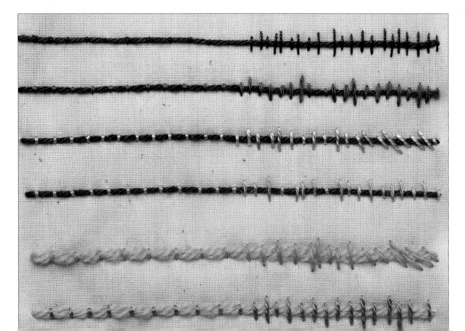

Couching stitch

Couching is ideal for outlining images and giving a raised line. Thick yarns that are difficult to work in a needle can be laid on the surface of the fabric and held down with a finer 'couching' thread, using short stitches at right angles. Try using a matching coloured thread for the couching stitches to blend in, or a contrasting colour for a bolder look. Vary the length and space between stitches for differing results.

Seeding stitch

Seeding is a variation of straight stitch created by working small stitches randomly in all directions. It is useful for filling backgrounds, flower centres, and textures like leaves and stones. This random grouping of stitches at different angles will resemble scattered seeds. Vary the length of the stitches and the weight of thread to see what effects are produced.

Fly stitch

This stitch is quite versatile and can be used singly or grouped together. Try varying the length of the stitch as you work. The stitches can form a line, be scattered randomly or used as a filling and are great for foliage effects. Fly stitch is worked easily since it is made up of a V-shaped loop which is then tied down by a vertical straight stitch. A longer straight stitch creates an extended fly stitch.

French knots

French knots can provide attractive surface textures. They can be worked individually or in loose or dense groups as a filling. Wrap your thread once round the needle for a perfectly circular knot or twice for a more irregular shape. I often work French knots quite loosely and this can give a more unusual appearance. Try using different thicknesses of thread as well as shiny and matt ones.

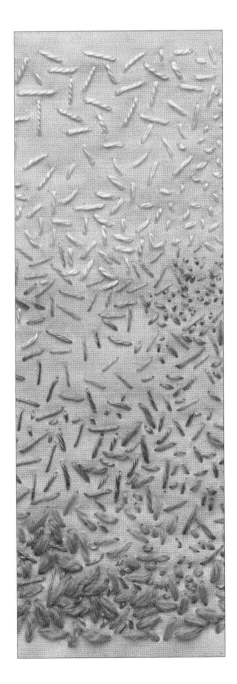
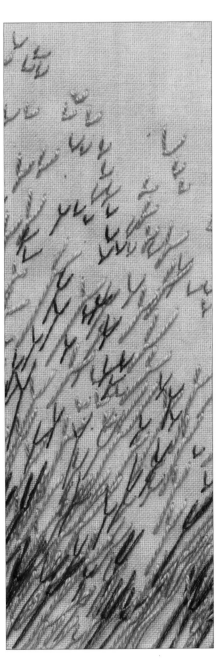
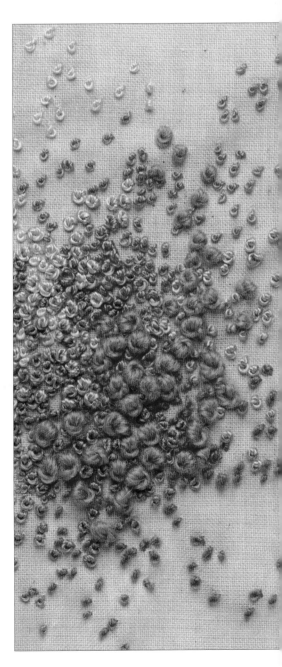

Cross stitch

Cross stitch can be worked quite randomly to create wonderful texture. Using a variety of weights and textures of thread you can work haphazard cross stitches, producing surfaces that resemble leaves on the forest floor or stubble in a cornfield as well as general backgrounds.

Combining stitches

As you explore the capabilities of these simple stitches you will start to create new and exciting surfaces. Remember that you are mark making and drawing with the thread. In the sample below I have combined French knots and seeding stitches. For the loose French knots I have worked with two threads in the needle. This gives a lovely effect, especially if they are different weights or shades.

Rusty Gate

This design is inspired by the colours and rusty textures of an ironwork gate (image page 17). I prepared a rust-dyed fabric background and made an acetate stencil for the ornate decorative feature. Xpandaprint was sponged through the stencil and heated with a hot-air tool. The surface was then worked into with hand stitching – couching to outline areas of the image and seeding and random cross stitch to emphasise the textured layers of rust.

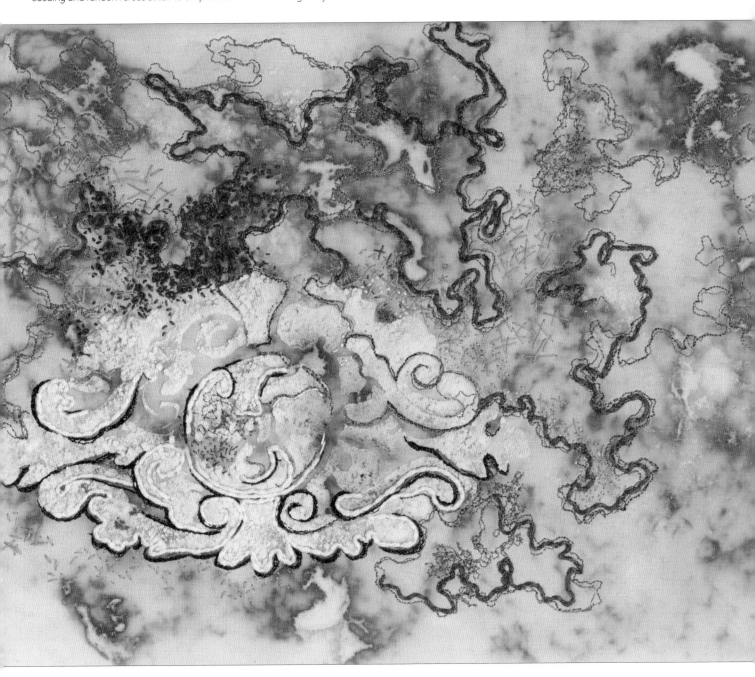

Playing with colour

Before embarking on any piece of work it is important to experiment as much as possible with a variety of techniques, materials and colour schemes. Only then will you be able to make really informed decisions about the best approach for each task. You can build up a range of samples before making your final choice. It is essential to play with colour so you can convey the correct mood and atmosphere and create a harmonious and pleasing design. Colour can be applied in a number of different ways, both in your sketchbook and on fabric, and here are some techniques for you to try. You will soon find the methods you prefer to work with.

Thick paints

Paints with a heavy consistency have great versatility. I like to use water-based fabric screen-printing inks which are thick and, consequently, suitable for all methods of application. Once applied to the fabric the colour can be fixed with heat by ironing for a few minutes. This will make the colour permanent and is therefore appropriate for any article that may require washing or damp-stretching before mounting and framing.

Mixing colours

These pigments are vibrant and can be mixed on a palette – I find white ceramic tiles perfect for this as they are easily cleaned afterwards. A palette knife is ideal for mixing the paints. When mixing paint colours it is important to always start with the lightest one. If creating the colour orange then start with yellow and gradually add the darker hue of red until you reach your desired orange. Keep testing on a spare piece of fabric while you mix as the 'actual' colour can be quite deceptive. Once you have achieved your chosen base colour you can then start to make lighter tints. Place some extender base on the palette and add the same amount of your orange mix, making the proportion 50/50. This will be lighter and you can then repeat the process. If you wish to make a darker shade then add minute amounts of black to your base colour. This will give you a range of colours that would be ideal for a monochromatic colour scheme. Instead of washing any excess pigment down the sink, use it to colour spare pieces of cloth. You could apply with a sponge, palette knife, or brush, or just wet a piece of fabric and use it to clean the palette, watching the colours mix and merge.

Using extender base

To create paler versions of colours but keep the same consistency, start with some extender base on your palette and then gradually add your chosen colour, again testing the colour on a spare piece of fabric. If you don't mix your colours too thoroughly, you can create some interesting effects when you apply them to the fabric.

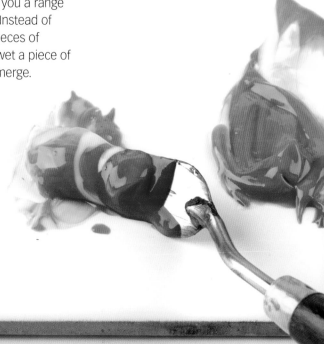

Overlaying colours

If the pigments you are using are translucent then you will be able to create interesting mixes on the fabric by overlaying colours. Experiment to see what colours you can create when you paint red or blue over yellow. Try using lighter and darker shades of each colour as you do this. Some overlays may give quite a muddy result so it is worth seeing what happens. If you are working with one colour and keep applying more and more layers, the effect will be much darker.

1 Take a piece of fabric and apply blocks of your primary colours: red, yellow and blue. I used a palette knife for this.

2 Once you have applied three blocks of each primary you can begin to overlay these colours, still using the primaries. Here I am applying red over yellow to create a more red-orange, then I will put red over blue.

3 Now work with blue and overlay the red, giving a blue-violet, and over yellow giving a green.

4 Laying yellow over blue gives a more olive-green, which is quite different to the green created in step 3.

Applying with a brush

You may prefer to use a paintbrush to apply thick paint, although you might need to add a small amount of water to the thick pigment so it gives a better coverage. Use a larger brush for covering large areas of your design and try not to keep overloading areas with paint as the colour may become too intense.

Applying with a palette knife

I like to use a palette knife and scrape the colour across the fabric. This can give some unexpected random effects and add to the free expression of your work. Pick up some paint on the edge of the knife, hold it at a 45° angle, then pull it towards you across the fabric. If your surface is made up of many layers and textures then the paint may not cover all the spaces as you scrape the palette knife across, so use a short, stubby paintbrush to fill in these areas if you want. Bear in mind that if you keep applying more layers of paint the colour may become too dark.

Applying with a sponge

Sponges are ideal for applying paint. Natural sponges give lovely textures and it is worth having a selection with different-sized holes. Using a dry sponge, work some paint on to it from the palette and then gently press down onto the fabric, leaving the impression. Turn the sponge at angles as you work across the surface, or drag it to create sweeping effects.

Diluted paints

Different effects can be achieved by diluting your paints or printing mediums. Water can be added in varying amounts – the more water you add, the lighter the colour will be. When you are working with a more diluted pigment it is less easy to control the flow, and bleeding may occur. This is not necessarily a bad thing – it just depends on the effect you wish to achieve. Some fabrics will be more absorbent than others, especially if they have been washed many times, like old sheeting, so you should experiment with a variety of fabrics to see what effects are produced. Allow your fabric to air dry before fixing the paint with an iron. If you try to iron it while still wet you will remove a lot of the colour – perhaps a good idea if your outcome is too dark!

Creating washes

1 Mix two different-coloured paints with water. I have used violet and sea green. Use a piece of pre-washed fabric and, working quickly with a brush, paint the top half. Adding more paint will make it darker; more water will make it paler. You can spray the fabric lightly with water before you begin.

2 Take your second colour and work into the bottom half, overlapping the green. The colours will start to merge and bleed into each other.

3 Use a water spray to create more merging of the colours.

4 When working with diluted paints, you can remove some of the colour by dabbing or stroking a paper towel onto the surface and soaking up some of the colour. This is an ideal technique for creating clouds.

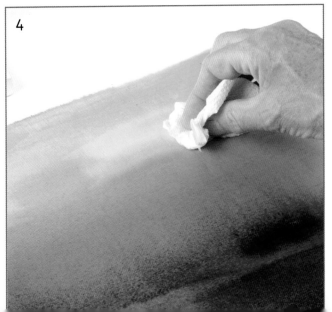

Using a textural background

Superb effects can be produced by applying diluted paint to a textured fabric background. In this sample a background has been created using a variety of natural fabrics, including calico, silk noil and cotton batting, which have been stitched with white cotton thread. This technique will be covered in the next chapter. The fibres in these fabrics have diverse properties and therefore accept the paint differently. By painting one colour across the different layers you can see that some will absorb it instantly and others will resist, creating variations of texture and tone.

Creating watermarks

When you are using diluted paints you can often create watermarks where the moisture spreads out across the fabric. This can be used to great effect in your designs, combining different colours and allowing them to merge. It can sometimes be frustrating though as the best watermarks often occur around the outside edge of your work! Try working on different fabrics and see what watermark effects you can achieve.

Creating reverse impressions

While you are experimenting with diluted paints it is a good idea to have spare fabric on hand, this could be curtain lining or old sheeting. Paint a piece of fabric and, while still wet, lay a second piece of plain, dry fabric on top. Press down gently and some of the colour will be absorbed. When you remove the top layer you will reveal some wonderful patterns.

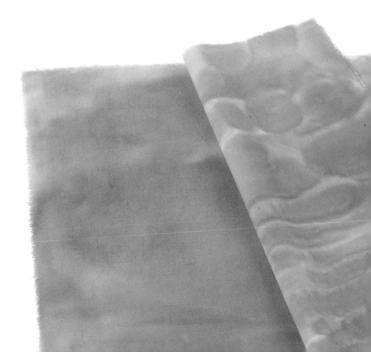

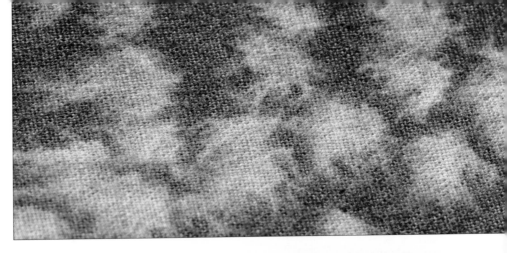

Salt resist

Using salt as a resist can create some beautiful results. Wet a piece of fabric and apply diluted paint. While it is still wet, sprinkle on some rock salt and leave flat to dry. The salt crystals will absorb the moisture from the paint, leaving light areas of pattern. Once dry, brush off the salt crystals and heat with a hair dryer to fix. You can then rinse the fabric to remove any salt residue. This technique works well on silk but experiment with other fabrics too.

Resist painting

There are various methods of resist printing and painting whereby the areas of the background fabric are prevented from taking on the colour of the paint. The simplest method is to tear or cut out shapes from masking tape or adhesive labels and stick them on to your fabric. Paint over the paper shapes and allow to air dry before removing them, then iron to fix. Do not add too much water to your pigment or it may seep under the edges of the paper.

Rust dyeing

The technique of rust dyeing is worth exploring. All you need are some rusty objects, water, salt and vinegar: water causes steel to rust and salt water speeds up the process. Try soaking nails, tin cans, wire wool, washers, wire, bolts and chains in a tray of salted water. Once the items have rusted you are ready to have fun. Use a pre-washed fabric – cotton sheeting or calico will do – and cut it into strips. Soak the fabric in basic malt vinegar with a little salt. Whilst still damp, wrap the fabric around your rusty object as tightly as you can, place in an old plastic bag and leave in a warm place. Do not seal the bag as the process needs oxygen. The fabric closest to the object will dye best. The longer you leave it the stronger the colour will be. You can then unwrap it and wash carefully to remove the vinegar and any rust 'bits'. Enjoy stitching into your rusty fabric!

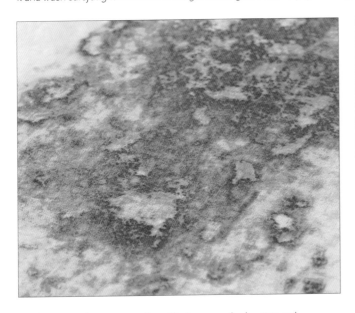

For this texture I wet some calico with vinegar and salt water and sprinkled it with shredded wire wool. Another piece of fabric was laid on top and the whole lot was left in a plastic bag in the sun. The result was a beautiful and richly coloured fabric.

This piece of calico was wrapped around a rusty tin can.

Block prints

There are some wonderful commercially produced printing blocks available on the market. These come in a wide range of designs but I find those with textured effects most useful. If you can't find quite the right print for your design you can easily make your own blocks from everyday objects, such as foam shapes, bubble wrap, sequin waste, screwed-up plastic bags – in fact anything with an interesting surface texture. You can fix small objects onto pieces of foam board or self-adhesive foam: try using matchsticks, washers, small twigs or string, all of which can make unusual blocks for printing. You must use a thick paint or printing ink for this technique.

1 Apply thick paint or printing medium to your printing block with a sponge or roller, keeping the coverage as even as possible.

2 Place your fabric onto a padded surface – a newspaper or thin blanket works well. Firmly press your printing block onto the fabric. You can make several prints with one application of paint but each one will be slightly paler. This can give a lovely aged or distressed look.

Stencils

Another way of applying pattern or texture to your design is to use a stencil. You can buy commercially produced stencils in a wide range of designs. However, it is fairly simple to make your own stencils from plain newsprint or similar paper. I prefer a torn edge when making paper stencils so I use a sharp clickers awl used for dressmaking with a comfortable wooden handle, and a long needle point. You could use the sharp point of a pair of compasses or a large needle instead. Working on a thick piece of card to protect the table surface I draw the stencil design onto the paper and then score along all the drawn lines, removing the shapes as I work. This method gives a much softer edge to the shapes as opposed to cutting with scissors. It is also easier to remove intricate shapes. Sequin waste, rug canvas and lace can also be used. Use small pieces of masking tape (rolled over to make it double sided and stuck to the back of the stencil) to hold the stencil in place. This helps to keep the stencil flat. You are then ready to apply the paint or printing medium using a sponge, stencil brush or even a palette knife for larger areas. Paper stencils can be ironed flat and re-used many times but if you want to create a more permanent design you can use a plastic acetate sheet and cut away the shapes using a soldering iron on a sheet of glass.

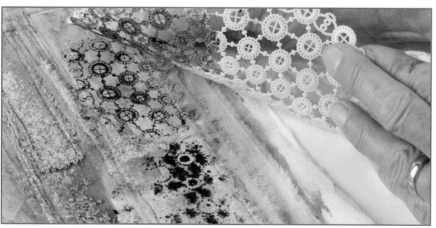

Printing and reverse printing

1 For this sample I am using a plastic doily, which has a beautiful pattern reminding me of stained-glass windows or fretwork. The stencil is placed in position on the background fabric and colour applied with a sponge through the holes. Lift the stencil carefully.

2 After the doily is removed it has paint on the surface so a reverse print can be made. Turn the stencil over and press down onto your fabric using a paper towel. You now have a positive and negative pattern from your stencil.

Using stencils and resists

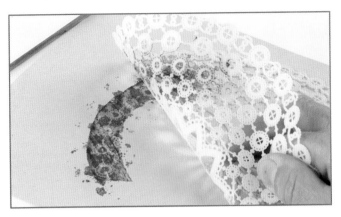

1 You may wish to apply your stencil pattern to a specific area of your design. To do so, you can mask out an area. I have cut out a curved arch shape from newsprint paper and positioned it on my fabric with masking tape. The stencil is then placed over the cut-out area of the mask and paint sponged through.

2 Lift off the stencil and paper mask to reveal the pattern in the required arch shape.

Choosing stencils and printing blocks according to the subject matter

When working with stencils and printing blocks it is important to select the appropriate effect for your piece of work. Sponges can be used to represent foliage or rock surfaces and the edge of a piece of card for grasses. Doilies and lace can replicate delicate carvings and mosaics. Some blocks and stencils create the characteristics of architectural features and carvings – Islamic geometric patterns, Celtic knot patterns and hieroglyphs. Sequin waste may be ideal for the scales on a fish. Be inventive and look around for objects to use in your work.

Playing with texture

I love looking at textures that are found all around us in nature, the landscape and architecture. When working in my sketchbook, recording ideas, I often build up layers of assorted papers to represent these different elements. I can then start to draw and paint into the raised surfaces. It is very important to experiment with a range of techniques so you can develop your own personal style and preferences. In this chapter I am going to encourage you to explore ways of creating surface textures with fabric, thread and three-dimensional media. I hope you will find some new ideas that will stretch you and make you question the use of different materials as you develop and combine these skills in your own work.

Selecting fabrics

These days there is a wide range of fabrics that you can explore and experiment with. By selecting and combining different textures you can create a huge variety of effects. You may wish to buy some fabrics but remember to keep your eyes open in charity shops and boot sales. Old tablecloths, sheets and even garments can be cut up and used. It is always best to wash your fabrics before use, especially if you intend to paint your textured surface or damp-stretch work before mounting and framing. Unwashed fabrics will still contain size or dressing and shrinkage may occur. As you are going to layer and stitch different fabrics together you do not want some to shrink and others not, distorting the finished piece. Look for fabrics with a variety of smooth, coarse and irregular textures. I like to use a selection of cottons, calicos, silk noil, cotton batting, linen, flannelette, scrim, crepe bandage, tape, lace and textured furnishing fabrics. Tearaway stabiliser can also be useful for layering.

Fraying fabrics

To add to the textured appearance of the design I try to tear my chosen fabrics whenever possible. Some just won't oblige though, and I have to cut first, keeping as straight to the grain as possible and then hand fray the edges. I would also choose to use scissors if my design requires a curved edge, perhaps the arch of a doorway or the peaks of a mountain.

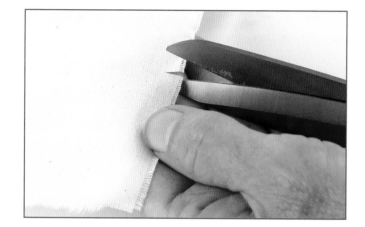

1 Snip the fabric with a sharp pair of scissors.

2 Hold both pieces of fabric either side of the cut and pull firmly apart. Think of the action as 'snip and rip'.

Layering fabrics

You can now enjoy selecting and layering your chosen fabrics. Use a piece of material as your background and then layer strips on top. Vary the widths and lengths of your pieces, keeping the heavier weights in the front. You might choose to use a landscape as your inspiration, keeping smooth, narrow strips of fabric towards the horizon and heavier, more textured layers in the foreground. Here I am using calico, silk noil, white cotton and cotton batting. I have incorporated a strip of selvedge from one of my pieces of linen, which has a lovely frayed edge.

Pinning and stitching fabrics

Once you are happy with the positioning of your fabrics you can pin them in place. Make sure you use plenty of pins or the fabrics may move out of position as you work. To prevent the work from puckering you should back it with a piece of tearaway stabiliser. Threading your machine with white or cream cotton thread, and using a darning foot, stitch around all your layered pieces, working 4mm (1/8in) from the edges, removing the pins as you go. Use a wooden skewer to help hold down fabric edges as you work. You may wish to add additional stitch texture using whip stitch or cable stitch at this stage.

Using three-dimensional fabric media

Products such as Xpandaprint or puff paint can produce surfaces that are ideal for representing moss, lichen, coral, rust and even crumbling stonework. They remain pliable once heated and are therefore suitable for stitching into. They will also take colour well, which means they can be blended into your background.

1 Use a dry sponge to apply the paste sparingly onto your fabric. Go gently to start with as it is easy to apply too much and end up with areas resembling cauliflowers on your fabric! Remember to wash your sponge before it dries out.

2 Working on a heat-proof surface, use a hot-air tool to heat the paste, holding the tool approximately 10cm (4in) away. Be patient as it may take a while for the crusty surface to appear.

Using horticultural fleece

Horticultural fleece is a thin, non-woven textile and can be purchased from garden centres. It is great to use in conjunction with fabric layers and stitching as it gives a random, textural element to your work. Its properties enable it to react with heat. Some nappy liners can be used in a similar way. Because heat will be applied for this technique you must make sure your fabrics are natural fibres, or your background may melt or singe.

1 Tear some horticultural fleece into small irregular pieces and place onto your background fabric. It can be applied before or after painting and gives a lovely cloud-like effect.

2 Sandwich your fabric between two layers of non-stick baking parchment, protecting both the ironing surface and the iron. Iron firmly for a minute or two.

3 Allow to cool and then remove the baking parchment. The fleece will now be adhered to your fabric. If the fleece lifts off the surface you should repeat the process, applying more heat. If you are applying it on to an unpainted background you can then apply colour, and the fleece will act as a 'resist'.

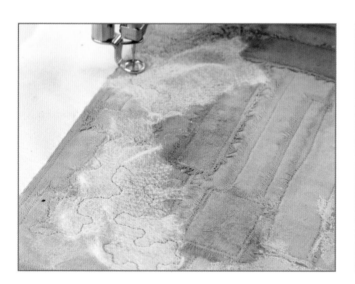

4 An alternative way to use the fleece is to apply it in small pieces to the background fabric, holding it in place with a random straight stitch.

5 Using a hot-air tool and working on a heat-proof surface, zap the fleece with bursts of heat, holding the tool about 10cm (4in) away from the surface. Once the fleece starts to react it will do so quite quickly, disintegrating into lacy patterns.

Texture gallery

Clockwise from top right:

I have used fabrics to create a variety of textures that could be used to denote architectural elements. The cuff from a lace glove suggests a balcony or balustrade and cotton tape is used for a column or window frame.

Some of these fabric edges have been torn and others cut and frayed. The selvedge edge of a piece of calico curls when it is stitched and a row of cable stitch provides further contrast.

Xpandaprint has been sponged on to layers of cotton batting and calico and then heated with a hot-air tool to give a wonderful texture suitable for rocks, moss, lichen or rusty surfaces.

Torn layers of calico and tearaway stabiliser with straight stitch and cable stitch.

This sample shows an area where horticultural fleece has been laid on top of cotton batting and stitched in place before zapping with a hot-air tool. This gives a beautiful raised surface texture.

In this sample, cable stitch has been worked on to the surface and then sponged with Xpandaprint and heated.

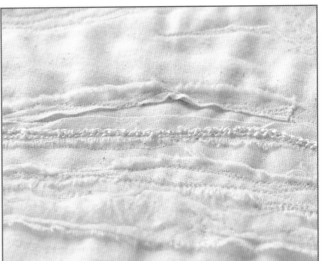

Design

We all encounter design in our everyday lives, in the carved detail of a church doorway, the placement of images and text on a poster, and the shape of beautiful ceramic objects. Being aware of our surroundings and recording ideas with cameras, phone cameras, notebooks and sketchbooks is something I am always encouraging my students to do. By looking at the different characteristics of objects, the colour shape and texture for instance, you can gradually learn to appreciate what you like and dislike. In order to use the multitude of wonderful techniques you have been experimenting with you will now need to make decisions about the design process itself. One method is to plan everything carefully in advance; starting with sketches and samples and following a step-by-step plan. In this way you can organise your ideas. A more spontaneous and experimental approach is to work with some initial ideas and thoughts and then let the plan evolve as you move elements around, discard some and keep working into it until you are happy with the result. Most of us will work somewhere between these two approaches.

Elements of design

Whatever medium you are working in, the fundamental aspects of design are the same and it is useful to be aware of the basic elements and principles.

Line is perhaps the most important element. Lines can be used to define shape, contours and outlines and can be continuous or broken. They can vary in width, length and direction and may be sharp and jagged, or fluid and smooth.

Shape is two-dimensional and defines the outline of an object. Positive shapes are the main subject areas of your design and the space around them creates negative shapes.

Form refers to objects that are three-dimensional, or have length, width and height.

Value, or tone, is the contrast of light and dark.

Space: the area around, above, and within an object is used to create the illusion of space. If objects overlap, the front shape will seem closer. Objects placed higher within the picture will appear further away as will smaller ones. Objects that are further away should have less detail and be cooler in colour temperature. They are also lighter in value, while objects that are closer are typically darker.

Colour is a strong design element that has an immediate impact on the viewer. The use of different colour harmonies can affect our moods and emotions (see page 18).

Texture is associated with the way things look or feel. There are many different kinds – rough, smooth, silky, matt, shiny, hard, soft, spiky, grainy and many more.

Principles of design

The principles deal with the way the elements are put together to create a composition.

Harmony pulls the pieces of a visual image together and can be achieved through repetition and rhythm. Patterns or shapes can help to create harmony.

Balance: this is the way in which the elements are arranged. It can be symmetrical, asymmetrical or radial.

Contrast creates excitement and interest. Two things that are very different have a lot of contrast like black and white or complementary colours like red and green.

Proportion: this refers to the relative size and scale of the different elements in a design and the relationship between them.

Focal point: the area that first attracts attention in a composition.

Rhythm is the repetition of elements in the design. This could be colours, shapes or patterns.

Movement: this is the path the viewer's eye takes through the artwork. It can be directed along lines, edges, shapes and colour.

The more you begin to understand these basic elements and principles the more confident you will become in planning and executing your designs. Mind maps can be an excellent way of exploring an idea or topic. Begin by writing a word that represents your initial thought. From that main idea create branches that each represents a single word relating to the main topic. Then create sub-branches that stem from the main branches to further expand on ideas and concepts. This will encourage you to think outside the box and explore topics from other viewpoints. It is also worth exploring ideas and images from different perspectives. Try to get close to the ground, look up or approach something sideways to discover an entirely new view. This can help to produce more original and visually interesting results. These are some of the methods I like to use when planning my own designs.

Computer-aided design effects

Designs and images can be adjusted and distorted by using photo-editing programs on the computer. I like to experiment with photographs that I have taken in order to look at the images in new ways, and use these as a basis for my designs.

Coloured–pencil effect.

Embossed effect.

Using drawings

Learning to draw means learning to see, and drawing from observation is the best way to really familiarise yourself with a subject. Try to draw from actual objects whenever possible so that you can truly absorb all the information, the shapes, changing light conditions, rich textures and details. Understanding how perspective works to give the illusion of space and distance is also important, with objects appearing to get smaller as they get further away.

   The most important thing to remember is to keep looking at what you are drawing and not record what you think it should look like. It is not always practical to have the subject matter in front of you so it is quite acceptable to work from photographs, but try to draw rather than trace the images. A white page in a sketchbook can be quite daunting so apply a colour wash over some pages before you begin, using inks, paint, tea or coffee. You can then begin to use a variety of drawing and painting techniques to record and experiment. Use different grades of pencil – hard and soft – charcoal, pastels and marker pens, as they will all create varying tones and thicknesses of line. Practise making marks that can be used to create texture and shading: stippling with dots, short dashes, hatching and cross hatching, wavy lines and scribbles. All of these marks can then be interpreted with stitch.

Using paper backgrounds

Creating surfaces with layers of paper can help you to visualise how you might interpret your ideas with fabric. I find it beneficial to construct textures in my sketchbook using a variety of techniques. Try tearing up strips of different textured papers, sugar, cartridge, tissue, wrapping, magazine and handmade papers, then layer and paste them using a glue stick or PVA adhesive. Or apply diluted PVA glue to a page and then press down screwed-up tissue paper to give a beautiful suede-like quality. These surfaces can then be coloured and worked into with drawing equipment.

Creating montages

When designing, consider combining a number of images relating to your topic in one composition. You can experiment by varying the scale and proportions of each element, perhaps enlarging a small carved detail and reducing the size of a large structure. Drawing each component onto separate pieces of tracing paper allows you to rearrange them until you are pleased with the end result. You can also see what happens when elements overlap each other. Consider the balance and harmony of your design as you are working.

1 Start by drawing a selection of images – I am using motifs taken from the work of the Spanish architect Antoni Gaudi – then enlarge or reduce the size of some using a photocopier. Using a translucent tracing paper or clear acetate sheets, copy these images using a black marker pen and start to arrange them into a balanced and pleasing design.

2 You can now add further details. Gaudi used lots of mosaic in his work so I am adding a section across the background.

Using paper collages

Paper collage is an ideal technique to use when planning a colour scheme. Try to build up a collection of different coloured papers to use for your collage. These papers can be torn, cut and layered to create a balanced and harmonious colour scheme.

1 Use a marker pen to draw your design onto tracing paper, making a note of which is the 'right side' of the image.

2 Select a range of coloured papers to represent your chosen colour scheme. These should show variation in tone from light to dark. Take one large piece of coloured paper and attach the tracing along the top edge with hinges of masking tape. You will now be able to keep raising the tracing as you position torn strips of paper in a balanced arrangement underneath.

3 Because you can see through the tracing paper you can rearrange the colours until you are satisfied. This doorway has a lot of vertical features so most of my paper strips are positioned to reflect that. I varied the width and length of the paper strips as I tore them.

4 You can now start to piece and layer coloured fabrics that correspond to the colours in your paper collage. The fabrics can be torn to give added textural interest. When this is done, the background is ready to stitch into.

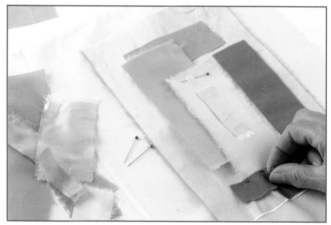

Enlarging your designs

Most of us have access to photocopying machines these days, in libraries, print shops and even at home. This makes it quick and easy to enlarge and reduce images when designing. For very large pieces of work an overhead projector is useful: you can draw onto an acetate sheet and then project it onto a large piece of paper attached to a wall.

Transferring your designs

For some designs you may wish to transfer all, or part of your image onto your fabric. There are a variety of methods you can use depending on your design or fabric colour, including fabric markers, tailors' chalk, pencil, dressmaker's carbon paper, transfer pencils and tearaway stabiliser. A light box can also be useful. Most of the time it is better just to work freely into your fabric without trying to follow specific marks and lines. However, if a design needs to be more precise my preferred method is to use a stabiliser and transfer the image from the reverse with stitch.

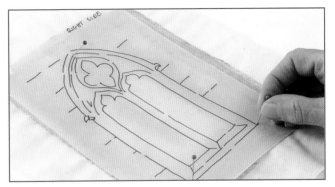

1 Trace your design onto tracing paper with a black marker pen and mark it 'right side'. Turn the tracing face down and lay on the table. Place a piece of stabiliser on top and copy the image using a hard pencil. This will be used to transfer the outline later, so keep it to one side.

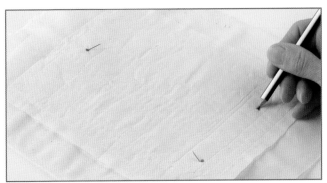

2 You now need to register the design so you can position the image on the reverse. Place your tracing 'right side' up on the front of your fabric and mark three or four dominant points with pins, pushing them through to the back.

3 Turn the fabric over and mark these pin points with a pencil or fabric marker on the back. Remove the tracing paper.

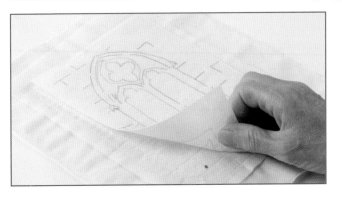

4 Now take your tearaway stabiliser tracing (which has been drawn in mirror image) and line it up with the marks, pinning in place. Your design will now be registered in the correct position ready to stitch. Thread your machine, top and bottom, with your chosen thread colour and start to stitch around the lines from the reverse. This will give you the basic outline on the right side of your work.

Displaying your finished piece

Once your paint has been heat-fixed and you have finished stitching your design, you can decide how to mount and frame it. Stretch your work out on a board covered with a damp cloth. Place it face up and attach with drawing pins, pulling it taut to remove any puckers that may have occurred while stitching. Spray lightly with water and leave to air dry. This process is called 'damp-stretching'. Once removed from the board, your design can be stretched over a piece of mount board or foam-board and laced up with strong thread on the reverse. This keeps it taut and gives a professional finish. It can now be surrounded by a card window mount and placed in a frame. Alternatively you could stretch your design over a canvas frame, or back it with fabric and keep as a soft hanging.

Flowers
Summer Meadow

Flowers are an endless source of inspiration for stitched textiles and provide continual pleasure for design. For this project you are encouraged to look at flowers growing in a cluster. I have chosen buttercups and daisies in a field. In this setting, flowers are viewed overlapping each other and the stems and grasses are swaying gently in the wind. Your stitch direction will create the effect of movement. A variety of fabrics are layered, stitched and painted and then worked into with freehand machine stitching. Be adventurous and create interesting surface texture before applying paint. You will see how you can incorporate broderie anglaise and flower lace trimmings as well as horticultural fleece and cable stitch to build up a rich surface before colouring it.

WHAT YOU NEED

GENERAL EQUIPMENT:

Sewing machine with darning foot or quilting foot

Embroidery scissors

Pins

Iron and ironing surface

Baking parchment

Fabric paints: extender base, Oxford blue, golden yellow and black

Brushes and palette knife

Wooden skewer

Masking tape

GENERAL MATERIALS:

Pre-washed calico

Selection of natural pre-washed textured fabrics such as silk noil and linen

Tearaway stabiliser

Broderie anglaise flowers

Flower lace trimmings

Horticultural fleece

Yellow organza fabric

White or cream cotton machine thread

White cotton perlé or crochet cotton for cable stitch

Coloured machine embroidery threads

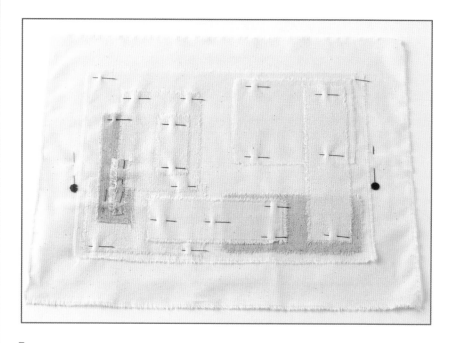

1 Take a piece of pre-washed calico, 40 x 30cm (15¾ x 11¾in), for the base. Cut a second piece, 30 x 20cm (11¾ x 7¾in), and place in the centre. Now start tearing your textured fabrics into strips and arrange them on the calico. Keep moving them around until you have a balance of shapes, tones and textures. For this summer meadow I have used mainly vertical strips of fabric as the flowers and foliage have an upright quality, with a few horizontals to give some contrast. Pin through all the layers. Pin your piece of tearaway stabiliser behind your base fabric to stabilise while stitching.

2 Set up your machine for freehand machine stitching and, using a darning foot and white or cream cotton thread, stitch the fabrics in place, keeping quite close to the frayed edges.

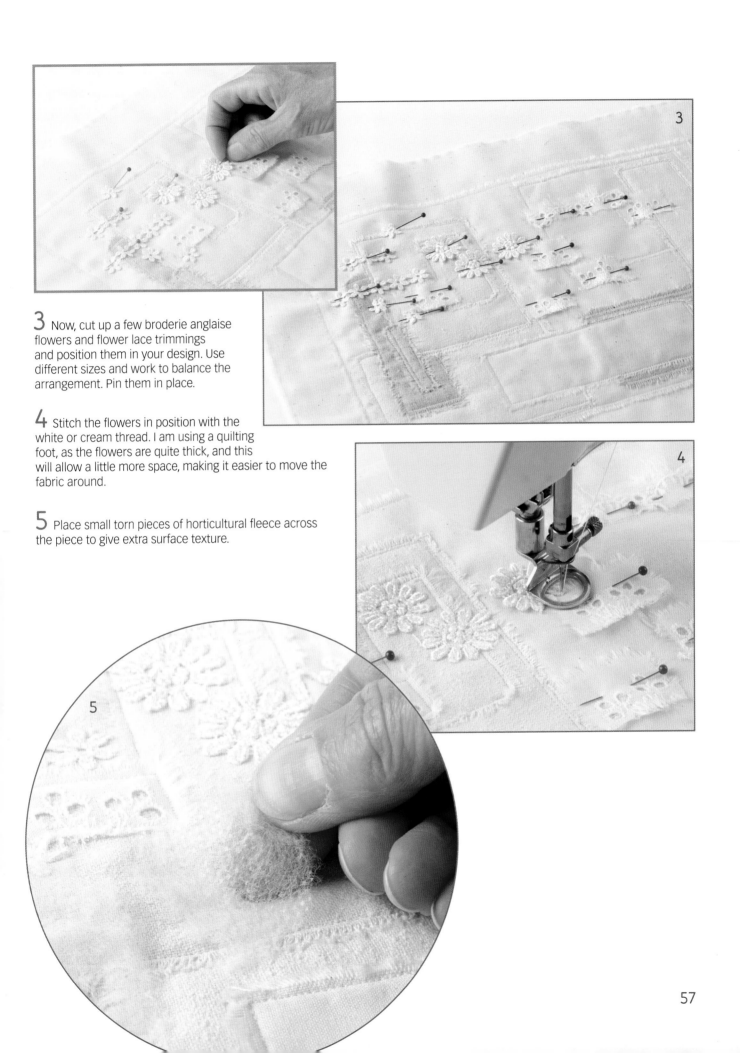

3 Now, cut up a few broderie anglaise flowers and flower lace trimmings and position them in your design. Use different sizes and work to balance the arrangement. Pin them in place.

4 Stitch the flowers in position with the white or cream thread. I am using a quilting foot, as the flowers are quite thick, and this will allow a little more space, making it easier to move the fabric around.

5 Place small torn pieces of horticultural fleece across the piece to give extra surface texture.

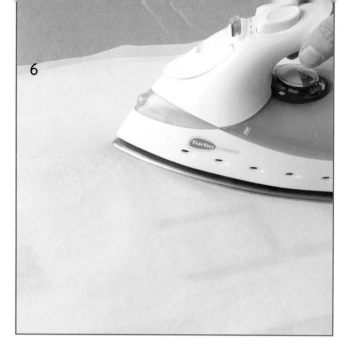

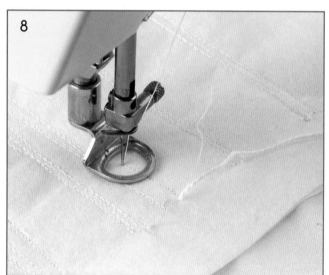

6 Cover with a sheet of non-stick baking parchment and, working on a heat-proof surface, iron across the areas of fleece. Remove the baking parchment. If the fleece has not adhered, repeat the process applying more heat.

7 You can now start stitching into the design, still using the white thread. Here I am stitching a few grasses and foliage.

8 Cable stitch can now be added. Fill the bobbin with cotton perlé, crochet cotton, or similar yarn. Turn your fabric over and, bringing the bobbin thread to the surface, start to stitch up and down, creating more grasses.

9 Your project now has a richly textured background with the cable-stitched grasses overlapping layers of fabric, flower lace trimmings, fleece and stitching.

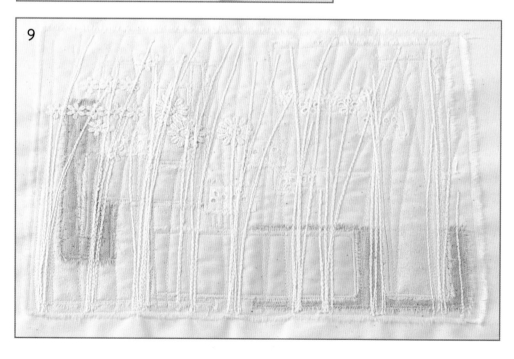

10

TIP

Attach masking tape around the edge of your design before painting to create a neat edge.

10 Mix a mid-blue paint (I have used extender base, blue and black) then apply the colour with a palette knife across the textured surfaces. You will find that the horticultural fleece will resist the paint and the fabrics and threads will take the paints in different ways, giving variation of tone and some surprising effects.

11 With a stiff paintbrush, work the colour into any gaps. You may need to add a small amount of water to ease the coverage, but try not to add too much extra paint. Vary the lower edge of the blue paint so you do not create a hard horizontal line. You will then be able to work into it with the second colour.

12 Mix your second colour (I have used extender base, golden yellow and blue) and fill in the lower half of the meadow using the palette knife.

11

12

13 Continue to work the green paint up to the blue and in some areas overlap it, balancing the colour as you work. Use the brush to fill in any gaps. Leave the paint to dry completely then iron to fix.

14 Now you can start to stitch with coloured threads, building up grasses and foliage. I am using a dark blue-green shade. Slant the direction of the grasses to create movement.

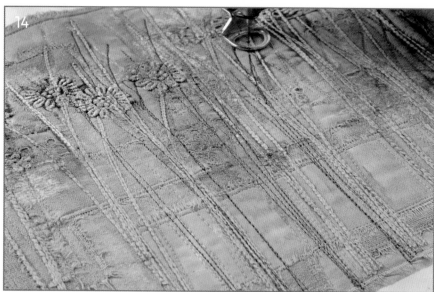

15 Stitch in some grass-like shapes. Variegated thread is ideal to give differing shades of ochre in these grasses. Remember to keep overlapping your stitching, creating layers. Stitch over some flowers and leave others prominent to create depth.

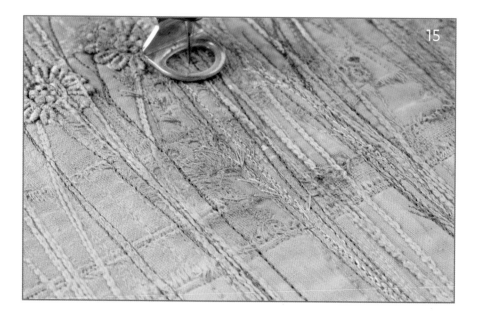

TIP
If areas of the work become quite dense you can increase your needle size.

16 Buttercups can now be added to the meadow. I am using two shades of yellow thread, one in the bobbin and one on top of the machine and adjusting the tensions to create a whip stitch (see page 27). To add extra texture I am applying small pieces of yellow organza fabric as I stitch the flowers, using a wooden skewer to hold them in place.

17 Work the daisies using a longer stitch length. To create this effect you should run the machine more slowly and move the fabric quickly, producing longer stitches. Some machines have an adjustable speed setting or you can just reduce the pressure you apply to the foot pedal. When you wish to move from one flower to another, remember to raise the presser-foot lever, move to the new position then lower it again making a few stitches to secure the thread (see page 22).

18 The flower centres are worked by moving the fabric around in short, quick circles, producing very small stitches. This result is known as granite stitch (see page 24). By using two different thread colours (yellow on the top and terracotta in the bobbin) and by tightening the top tension you can achieve a lovely effect. Keep working on the picture until you are happy with the effect. You can add some hand stitching too, if you like.

You can see how rich the surface texture has become. The flower lace trimmings and broderie anglaise add depth to the background and there is contrast between the small stitches in the buttercups and the longer, smooth stitches for the daisy petals. Using a combination of techniques and altering the stitch length generates interest.

The painted rows of cable stitch contrast well with the lines of straight stitching for the grasses. The yellow organza behind the buttercups provides a shimmer effect and additional texture.

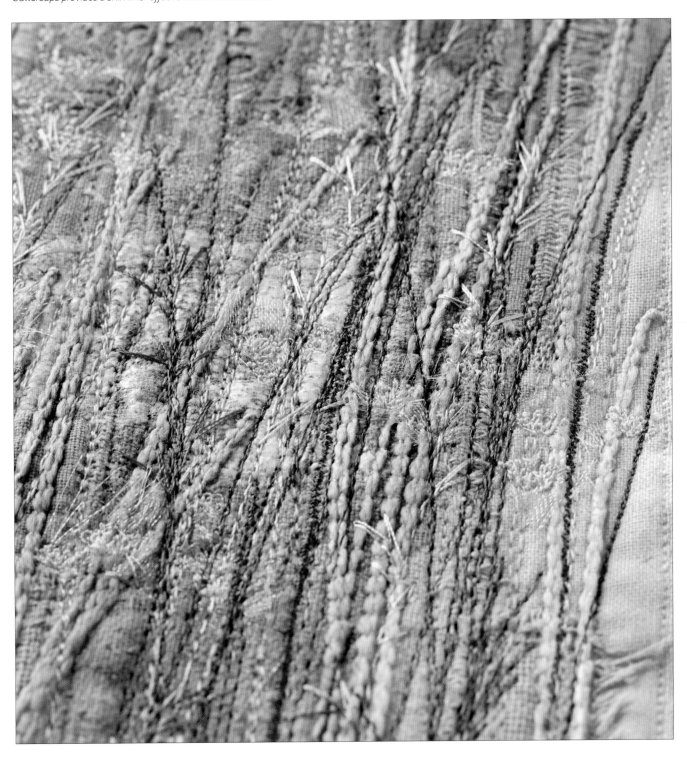

The granite stitch in the centre of the daisies contrasts with the longer stitch length of the petals. The horticultural fleece can be seen in the top section of this detail and it gives a random, distressed look to the surface.

The clusters of buttercups are built up using different shades of thread. The broderie–anglaise flowers show textural contrast but at the same time blend in to the painted background.

Consider the spaces between elements in your work. The background does not have to be covered in stitching. You have lovely textures from the frayed, stitched and painted fabric strips, so make sure you allow these to be shown to their best advantage between the rows of stitching.

Iris

Everyone must have a favourite flower. I have several favourites and the iris is one of them. For this project, think about the beauty and detail of individual flowerheads. You may choose to use a different flower altogether for your design but you can still follow the techniques and processes. Drawing from observation is the best way of understanding the structure, shape and textures of your chosen flower so do take time to really study it with care. Take photographs and record the colours in your subject. Look at the number of petals and how they grow in relation to each other. Are the veins in the petals dominant or quite faint? How do the petals curl or bend as they extend from the flower centre. What colours and textures can you see in the centre of the flower? Irises have three sepals that droop downwards, often patterned with small hairs or beards or with veining, lines or dots. Their three petals stand upright in the centre. Look at how the buds of your flower are formed. All these studies will give you a greater awareness when you come to interpret your flower in textiles.

In this project you will layer natural fabrics, build up texture with machine and hand stitching and colour the background with fabric paint. Fine chiffon scarves are used to create texture for the flowers and buds, and then the project is stitched into with coloured machine embroidery threads incorporating whip stitch using nylon invisible thread. Have fun creating your own design, inspired by your favourite flower.

WHAT YOU NEED

GENERAL EQUIPMENT:

Sewing machine with
 darning foot

Embroidery scissors

Pins

Hand embroidery needle

Iron and ironing surface

Fabric paints: extender base,
 azure blue and green (mixed
 with blue and yellow)

Brushes and palette knife

Wooden skewer

Tracing paper

Pencil and marker pen

Masking tape

Paper and paints or pastels

Coloured papers and glue stick
 for collage (optional)

GENERAL MATERIALS:

Pre-washed calico

Selection of natural
 pre-washed textured
 fabrics such as silk noil
 and white cotton

Tearaway stabiliser

Blue, purple, brown and beige
 nylon chiffon scarves

White or cream thread or yarn
 for hand stitching

White or cream cotton
 machine thread

Nylon invisible thread

Tacking thread

Coloured machine
 embroidery threads

1 Draw your flower and copy onto tracing paper using a black marker pen. Mark the right side of your tracing. See page 53 for further advice on enlarging and transferring designs. Turn the tracing face down on the table and trace the image onto one piece of tearaway stabiliser, using a hard pencil. Keep to one side.

2 Tear a piece of calico – approximately 25 x 40cm (9¾ x 15¾in) – for your backing and then a smaller piece to place in the centre (this will be the size of your finished picture). Position the tracing, right side up on to the centre piece of calico and attach along the top edge with hinges of masking tape. You will now be able to raise and lower the tracing as you position torn strips of fabric in a balanced arrangement underneath.

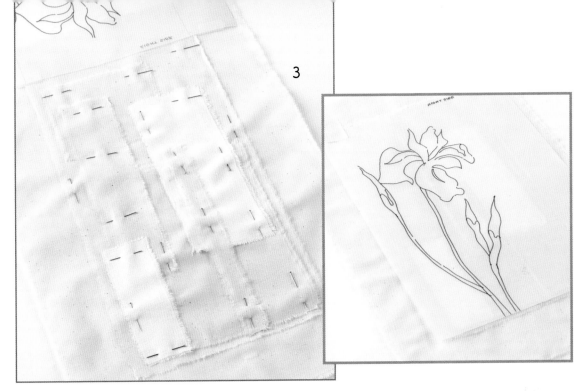

3

4

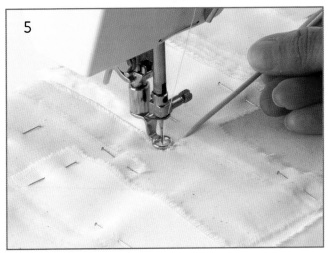

5

6

3 Due to the nature of the image, I have kept my strips of fabric mainly vertical but varied the lengths and widths. When you lower the tracing on top of the layered fabrics you can see how they look in relation to the elements of the design. When you are satisfied, pin them all in place.

4 Take the second, plain piece of tearaway stabiliser and pin behind your design.

5 Set up your machine for freehand machining and attach a darning foot. With a white or cream cotton thread stitch the fabrics in place, keeping quite close to the frayed edges. Remove the pins as you work and use a wooden skewer to help keep down any awkward corners.

6 You may find it easier to lift some of the upper fabric strips and secure the lower layers, before re-positioning and stitching on top. In most areas you can just stitch the top layers, which will automatically hold down those below.

7 The frayed edges of your torn fabrics give a lovely depth and texture to the surface and the different tones provide background variation.

8 Using white or cream thread or yarn, work into the background with some hand stitching. I am working vertical rows of straight stitch to suggest stems or stalks.

9 To plan your colour scheme, work on paper with paints or pastels, or create a paper collage (see page 52). By laying your tracing paper on top you can balance the colours as you work.

10 Apply masking tape to the edges of your design in preparation for painting. Now mix fabric paints for your colour combinations. With your colour sketch or collage alongside, start to apply the paint to your fabric, using a palette knife or brush.

11 With a paintbrush and a small amount of water, gradually work into any gaps, spreading the paint to give an even coverage. Lift up the frayed edges to ensure the fabric underneath is coloured.

12 Blend and overlay the colours where they meet to give a softer look. When the paint is dry, remove the masking tape and iron to fix.

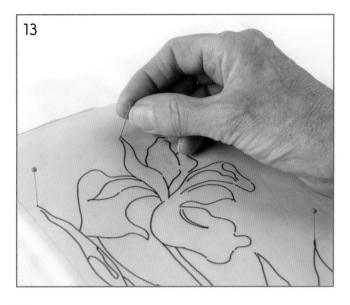

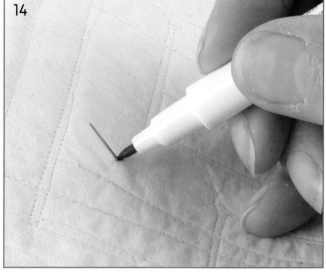

13 The next step is to register your design on the reverse in order to transfer the image and apply the chiffon. Re-position the tracing 'right side' up on top of your painted fabric. Mark three or four dominant points with pins, pushing them through to the back of the fabric.

14 Turn the fabric over and mark these pin points with a pencil or fabric marker. Remove the tracing paper.

15 Now take your tearaway stabiliser tracing (which has been drawn in mirror image, see step 1) and line it up with the marks, pinning in place. Your image will now be registered in the correct position, ready to stitch.

16 To apply blue chiffon for the main flower, place a double layer on the surface of the fabric, then pin and tack in place.

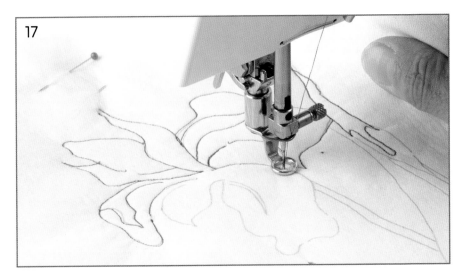

17 Thread your machine, top and bottom, with dark blue thread and, from the wrong side, start to stitch around the shapes of the flower and buds. This will transfer the basic outline on to the right side of your work and attach the chiffon.

18 Remove any tacking threads and trim away the surplus chiffon, giving a soft, semi-transparent layer of colour over the flower and buds.

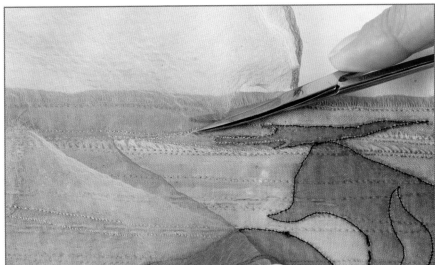

19 Now repeat the process for the stems. I have used two layers of chiffon, brown and beige. Pin and tack in place, stitch from the reverse and then trim away the surplus.

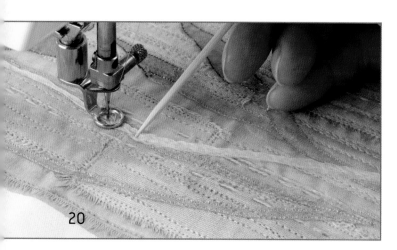

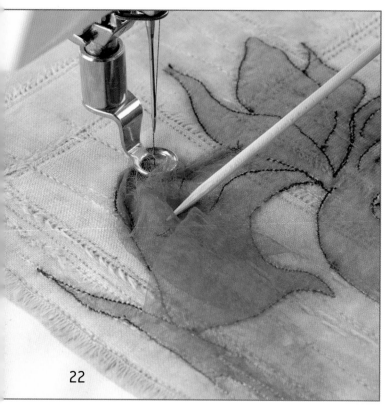

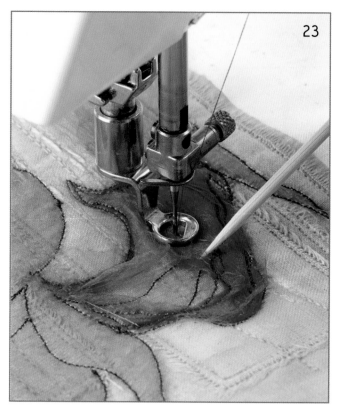

20 You are now going to work with more coloured threads. I am using the cut, seam edge of the chiffon scarf and a beige thread to apply it to the stems using a straight stitch. Use your wooden skewer to help hold it in position as you work.

22 You can now start to add extra depth of colour to the flowers by applying pieces of blue chiffon with straight stitching, taking into account your stitch direction and using it to add extra sketchy detail to the petals. Use the skewer to manipulate it as you progress.

21 Add further lines of stitching next to your chiffon stem. This gives a denser colour and a more raised texture. The straight stitching will create an irregular shadow effect.

23 Vary the density of the layers of chiffon to give added interest and shading.

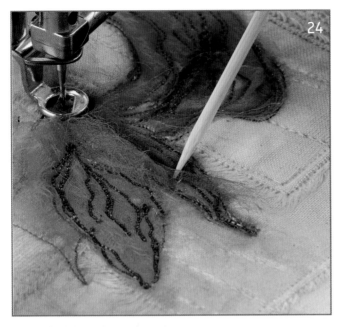

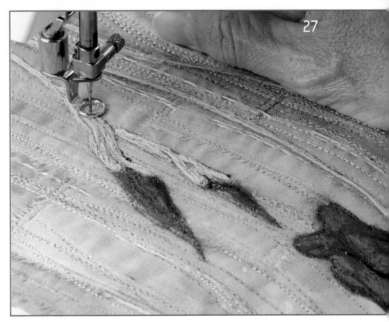

24 For the centre, upright petals I have applied some purple and blue chiffon. Try not to overstitch – allow the chiffon to have some space around it.

26 I am now adding a second colour on top. This purple reflects the purple chiffon in the petals.

25 Now you can create some beautiful raised texture for the iris beards. Use a clear nylon invisible thread on the top of the machine and tighten the top tension. Filling the bobbin with your chosen colour, work whip stitch, pulling the bobbin thread onto the surface (see page 27). If the thread does not pull through enough, loosen the bobbin tension.

27 Continue stitching, adding more chiffon and background grasses until you are satisfied with the result. Remember to look at your work from a distance every now and then to check that you are keeping everything balanced.

The use of fine nylon chiffon allows you to vary
the tone within areas of your work. Edges can be
softened and, by manipulating the chiffon, you
can create a subtle texture. In this detail you can
see how the tall, upright petals have more layers,
making them denser and much darker. The outer
edges of the lower sepals are paler with fewer layers.

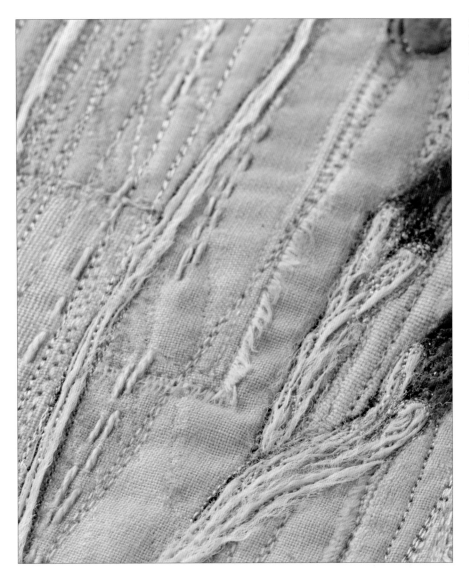

The rolled edge of a nylon chiffon scarf is ideal for the stems and the buds, giving extra depth. The straight stitching, worked by hand before painting, blends in with the background layers. It provides texture but, having picked up the colour of the paint, it merges with the fabric.

The chiffon used in the buds and stalks is a lovely contrast to the woven fabric and stitching underneath.

This really shows how effective whip stitch can be. It has produced a rich, crusty texture that rises up above the surface of the sepals, replicating the way the short hairs of an iris beard emerge. It is a stitch well worth practising as it offers so many possibilities.

The vertical nature of this composition can be seen here. The torn edges of the fabric strips, the hand stitching, the bands of colour and the machine stitching all allow the eye to follow the stems up to the detail of the flower itself.

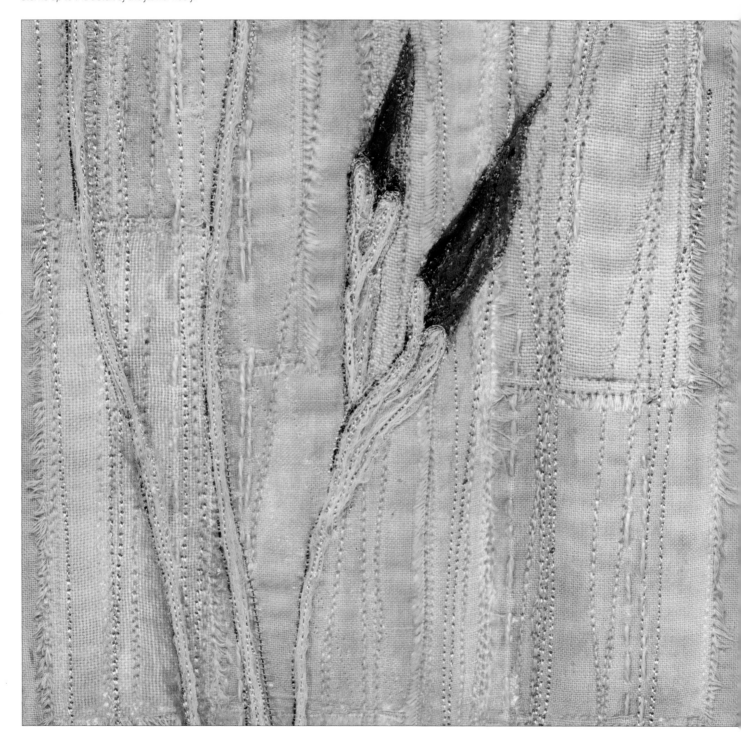

Flowers gallery

Tulip

25 x 47cm (9³/₄ x 18¹/₂in)

Layers of paper and fabric make up the background for this design. Heavy-weight interfacing was used as a base and I covered it with a layer of transfer adhesive. After peeling off the backing paper, torn paper pieces and screwed-up tissue paper were applied and ironed in place. Additional texture was added using scrim and blocks of heavy-weight interfacing, hand stitched in place with straight stitches and seeding. The background was then coloured with diluted fabric paint before stitching the tulip. Red organza was applied in layers and distressed with a soldering iron.

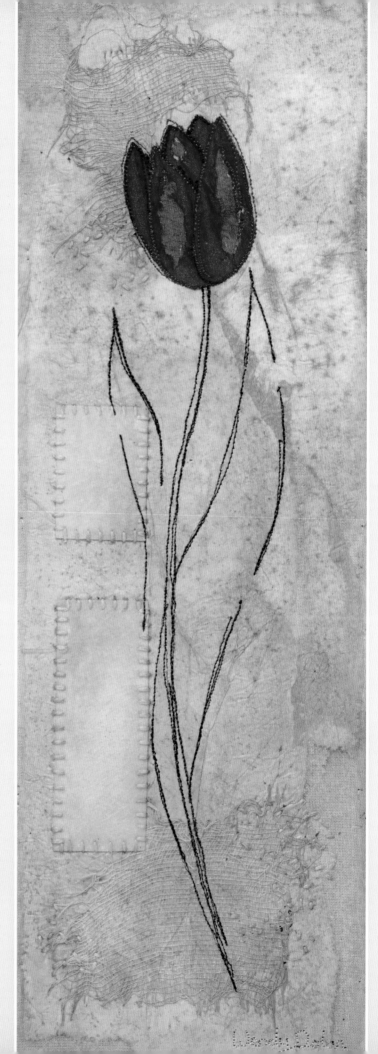

Bluebell Time

32 x 53cm (12½ x 20¾in)

*Ashdown Forest in Sussex
is a wonderful source of
inspiration at any time of year.
In spring however, the vista is
spectacular when bluebells
cover areas of the forest floor
like blankets. It is a favourite
place of mine to sit and sketch
and to take photographs.
Bluebell Time is a result
of several forest visits and
sketches developed back in
my studio. Calico and silk noil
have been torn, pieced and
patched, building up horizontal
and vertical layers suggesting
grass and trees. The effect of
sunlight through the trees and
swathes of bluebells was then
captured by using fabric paints.
Foliage has been stitched
before I added painted fabric
strips for the trees and applied
further stitching.*

Architecture

Venetian Window

Architecture offers artists a wealth of design opportunities. Doors, windows, arches and carved details can all be researched and developed into inventive works of art. Venice is a magical city that never ceases to provide ideas for my artwork. For this project I have selected a window taken from one of the most beautiful buildings in the municipality, the Ca' d'Oro palace, the house of gold. The main facade overlooking the Grand Canal boasts an assortment of columns, arches, balconies and quatrefoil windows, in the Gothic style. This project explores the contrast between the beautiful decorative qualities of the architecture and the crumbly nature of the stonework where the walls are weathered. Fabrics and lace trimmings are pieced and layered, building up the surface, with additional texture created with horticultural fleece and a three-dimensional fabric medium such as Xpandaprint or puff paint. Fabric paints are used to colour the background and then the design is transferred and worked with machine stitching, including cable stitch. You may wish to select a favourite doorway or church window for your piece but try to choose one with contrasting textures.

WHAT YOU NEED

GENERAL EQUIPMENT:

Sewing machine with darning foot

Embroidery scissors

Pins

Wooden skewer

Iron and ironing surface

Hair dryer

Baking parchment

Hot-air tool

Fabric paints: extender base, Oxford blue and terracotta (mixed with yellow, red and black)

Xpandaprint or puff paint

Brushes, sponge and palette knife

Tracing paper, pencil and marker pen

Coloured papers

Glue stick

Masking tape

GENERAL MATERIALS:

Pre-washed calico

Selection of natural pre-washed textured fabrics such as silk noil, linen and cotton scrim

Tearaway stabiliser

Lace trimmings

Horticultural fleece

White or cream cotton machine thread

Coloured cotton perlé or similar yarn for cable stitch

Coloured machine embroidery threads

1 Select your design source and draw it as a simplified line drawing. Copy the image onto tracing paper using a marker pen and mark the 'right side' of your tracing. Turn the tracing face down and lay on the table. Place a piece of tearaway stabiliser on top and copy the image using a hard pencil. This will be used to transfer the outline later, so keep it to one side.

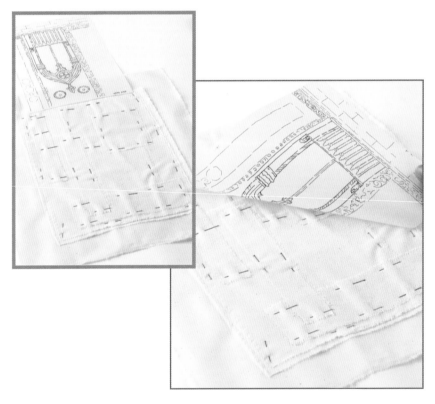

2 Take a piece of calico slightly larger than your image size and place it on a larger piece of calico for the backing. Position the tracing, 'right side' up onto the centre and attach along the top edge with hinges of masking tape. You will now be able to raise and lower the tracing as you position torn strips of fabric in a balanced arrangement underneath. Vary the textures, widths and lengths of the fabric strips and position according to the concept – vertical where there are columns, window or door frames and horizontal for balconies and window ledges. Pin in place. Attach a piece of stabiliser behind the work with a couple of pins.

3

4

5

3 Stitch down the fabric strips using white or cream cotton thread. Lay small pieces of loosely woven scrim in areas where there may be 'weathering' and use a wooden skewer to help hold these in place while you stitch. Small areas of horticultural fleece can also add to the texture. Iron fuse in place using baking parchment (see page 46).

4 Xpandaprint or puff paint can now be added for crumbly wall texture. Try not to overload your sponge with the paste.

5 Gently apply the Xpandaprint or puff paint to the required areas. They are very effective if applied over scrim and frayed fabric edges. Wash the sponge after use.

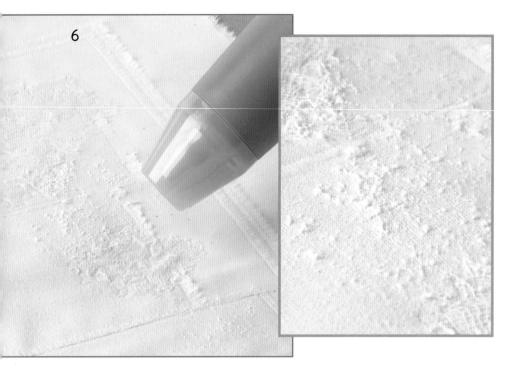

6 Working on a heat-proof surface, use a hot-air tool to heat the paste, holding the tool approximately 10cm (4in) away from the fabric. Be patient as it may take a while for the crusty results to appear. You will see interesting effects where the scrim shows through.

7 You can now apply pieces of lace to represent carved details on your design. In order to place these trimmings accurately, replace your tracing and position the lace underneath.

8 Take an assortment of papers according to your colour scheme and create a collage. Tear the papers into strips and arrange them on a piece of backing paper with the hinged tracing on top (see page 52).

9 Raise and lower the tracing until you are happy with the balance of your colours, then paste the papers down.

10 You are now ready to paint your background, using the paper collage as a reference. Mix all your colours first so you can work fluently and then apply the colour with a palette knife or brush. As you scrape the knife across the surface, the Xpandaprint or puff paint applied in step 5 will slightly resist the colour, giving lovely effects.

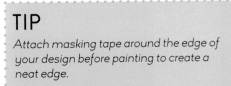

TIP
Attach masking tape around the edge of your design before painting to create a neat edge.

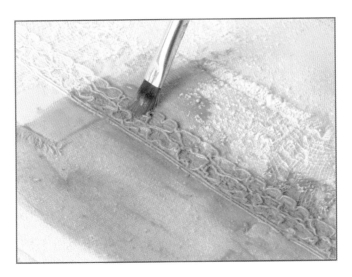

11 You may need to use a small, stiff brush to ensure the paint covers textured areas of lace and scrim sufficiently. Use a hair dryer to fix the paint so the raised areas are not spoilt.

12 You will be transferring the image by stitching from the reverse, so you now need to register the design. With the tracing 'right side' up, place in position on your painted fabric and mark three or four dominant points with pins, pushing them through to the back. Turn the fabric over and mark these pin points with a pencil or fabric marker on the reverse (see page 53). Now take your tearaway stabiliser copy of the image (from step 1) and line up the pencil marks with the relevant points. Pin in place.

13 Thread your machine with a dark colour in the bobbin and on top. You can now start to stitch the design from the back; the bobbin thread will create the outline on the right side of the fabric. When you come to a short gap in the lines, move across to the opposite side of the design, as shown, and continue stitching, as it is easier to trim long threads.

14 Every now and then turn to the right side, trim the threads and check your tensions are correct.

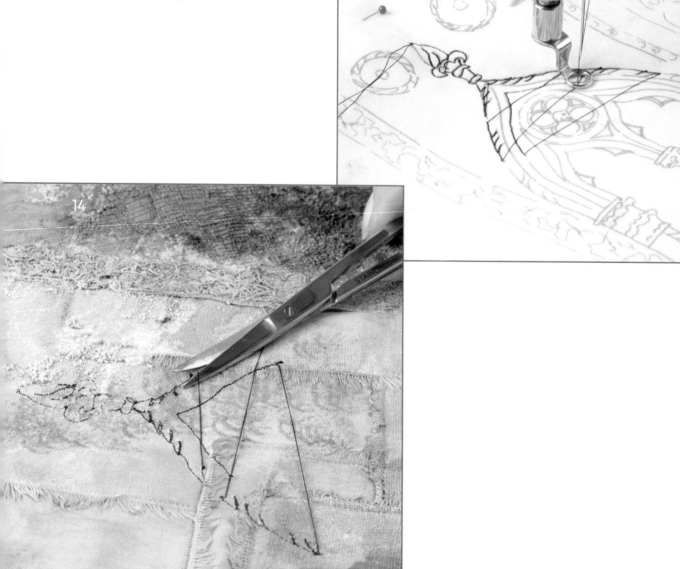

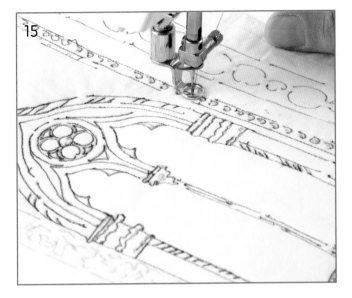

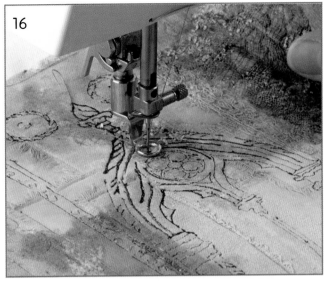

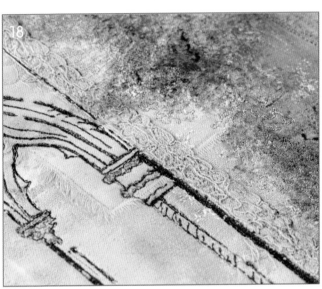

15 You may wish to change thread colour as you work on different areas.

17 Cable stitch is ideal for carved accents, giving surface interest and texture (see page 28). I have used blue cotton perlé in the bobbin.

16 With the lines transferred onto the painted surface you can now begin to work on the right side. Use threads that are relevant to your colour scheme and start to add emphasis to certain areas. Several rows of straight stitch can accentuate lines, as well as narrow satin stitch. Here I am highlighting some of the window arches with terracotta thread.

18 Carved details on the columns and capitals are worked with straight stitch. Remember to keep viewing your work from a distance as you proceed with your stitching, to check the effects.

TIP

If you feel your picture needs a little lift, add complementary colour, as I did with the terracotta thread (see page 18).

The cable stitch gives a beautiful raised texture for these carved accents. The use of horticultural fleece gives a distressed look to the wall with the addition of closely worked granite stitch. By not stitching all the lines completely you can maintain a sketchy feel to your work.

Different shades of blue thread give variation to the image and the use of the complementary colour – orange – for the highlighting provides a strong contrast.

This detail shows how the corded lace trim perfectly represents a carved column. Xpandaprint, scrim, paint and stitch combine to provide a rich, distressed texture for the wall.

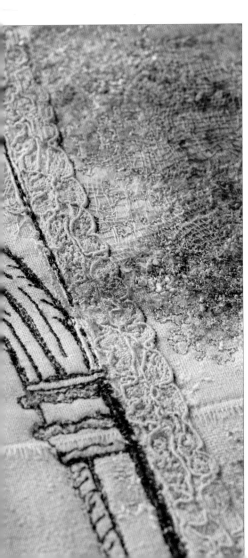

The torn and frayed edges of the fabric give
a lovely random surface effect, as do the
contrasts between the different layers of silk noil
and calico. The use of narrow satin stitch on the
left-hand side and lower edge of the balcony
gives a bold definition to this feature.

A combination of textures can be seen in the detail of the quatrefoil window. You may choose to leave some lines quite fine and delicate in contrast to bolder outlines, giving a three-dimensional effect.

Montage Inspired by Gaudi

If you have been fortunate enough to visit Barcelona, you will no doubt have come across the unusual and quirky buildings and masterpieces of the architect Antoni Gaudi. He was inspired by nature and used flowing lines and curves in his work. Chimneys were constructed using extraordinary forms and human bone shapes were used for columns, staircase banisters and balconies. Mosaic patterns adorn many of his structures and they contrast with areas of smooth stonework. Stained-glass windows with metalwork grids offer wonderful ideas for design.

For this project I have selected different elements from Gaudi's work and created a montage of images. Chimneys from the Casa Mila and Palau Güell are combined with mosaic patterns from Parc Güell benches and a metal grid from a window in the Colònia Güell crypt. The images have been enlarged, reduced and re-arranged to create a cohesive composition, using tracing paper (see page 51).

Techniques include tearing and layering fabrics and applying horticultural fleece. Sheer fabrics are applied to add surface interest and a variety of mosaic effects using stencilling and applied fabrics are explored. Freehand machine stitching adds line, form, detail and texture.

WHAT YOU NEED

GENERAL EQUIPMENT:

Sewing machine with darning foot

Embroidery scissors

Pins

Iron and ironing surface

Baking parchment

Fabric paints: extender base, mid-brown, sea green and fuchsia

Brushes, sponge and palette knife

Wooden skewer

Paper doily

Coloured papers

Tracing paper, pencil and marker pen

Glue stick

Masking tape

GENERAL MATERIALS:

Pre-washed calico

Selection of natural pre-washed textured fabrics such as silk noil and linen

Tearaway stabiliser

Iron-on transfer adhesive (optional)

Horticultural fleece

Coloured sheer fabrics such as organza and net

White or cream cotton machine thread

Coloured cotton perlé or similar yarn for cable stitch

Coloured machine embroidery threads

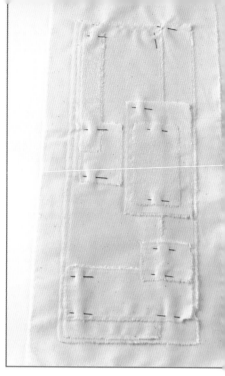

1 Create your design using a montage of images (see page 51) and copy onto tracing paper with a marker pen, marking the 'right side'. Take a piece of pre-washed calico, slightly larger than your image size and place it on a larger piece for the backing. Position the tracing, 'right side' up onto the centre and attach along the top edge with masking tape to form a hinge. You can now begin to tear your fabrics into strips and arrange them according to your plan. Pin in place. Cut two pieces of tearaway stabiliser, using one to copy your design in mirror image (see page 53) and set to one side.

2 Pin the second, plain piece of stabiliser behind, to strengthen the work, and machine stitch all your fabrics in place using white or cream cotton thread.

3 Tear small pieces of horticultural fleece and position across select areas of your design. Cover with baking parchment and iron to fuse in place (see page 46).

5 You now need to register your design on the back. Place the tracing paper on the right side and mark three or four points with pins. You can then line up the tearaway stabiliser on the reverse (see page 53).

4 Plan your colour scheme by creating a paper collage (see page 52) and then apply masking tape to the edges of your work in preparation for painting. Mix your paint colours. Apply the paint with a palette knife or brush using the paper collage as reference. Iron to fix, using baking parchment to protect the areas where you have used horticultural fleece.

6 From the wrong side, stitch around the main elements through the tearaway stabiliser, transferring the lines. Remember, it is the bobbin thread that will be visible on the right side, so choose your thread colours carefully, making sure they are bold enough to show.

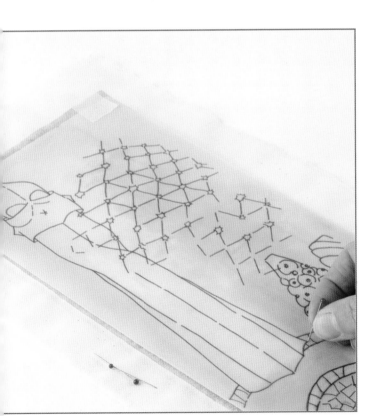

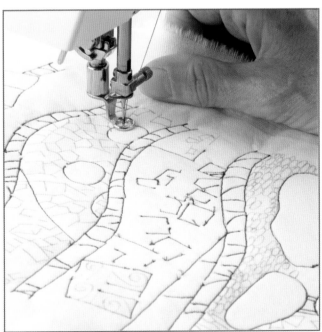

7

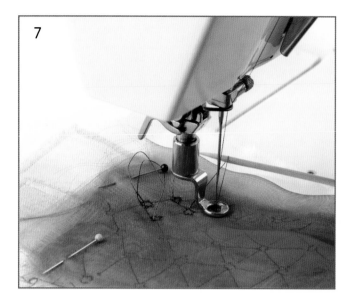

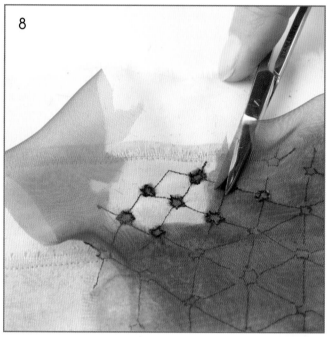

TIP

When shapes are close together, raise the presser-foot lever and pull through the top thread with your wooden skewer, before lowering the lever and stitching the next shape. This will make it easier to cut the joining thread.

8

7 To apply small pieces of fabric to specific areas of your work, use the cut-away appliqué method. Pin or tack a large piece of fabric over the design area – I am using a purple organza. Stitch around the shapes you wish to cover with the fabric, using a short stitch length.

8 Trim away the excess fabric around the shapes. Curved-tip embroidery scissors are ideal for this.

9 Once you have outlined the main elements you can continue stitching from the right side, emphasising lines and shapes and adding details and textures. Add further decoration as explained opposite until you are happy with the result.

9

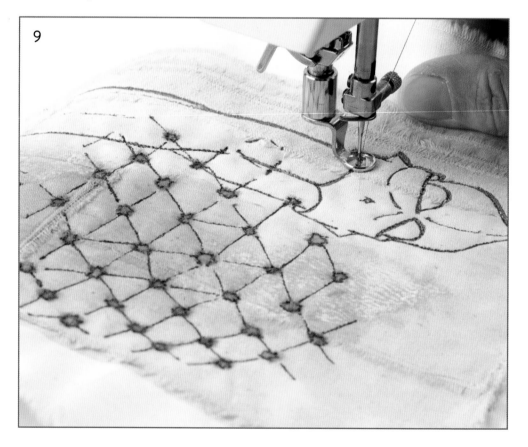

Mosaic techniques

Gaudi incorporated a lot of mosaic work in to his architecture and there are many ways you can achieve similar effects with fabric, paint and stitch. Try a few of these methods to add detail to your work.

Apply small pieces of coloured fabrics to your background. These could be secured with transfer adhesive first or held down with a wooden skewer as you stitch. Add lines of stitching around the shapes and across the background. Here I have added granite stitch between the shapes for extra texture.

Work shaky zigzag over areas of the mosaic (see page 25), merging it into the background. If this is done with a silky thread it adds shimmer as well as texture to the design.

Paper doilies are ideal for stencilling mosaic patterns. To apply the pattern to a particular section of your work, cut a hole in a piece of paper to the required shape and hold in place with masking tape. Lay the doily over the exposed area of fabric and then apply layers of paint with a sponge.

 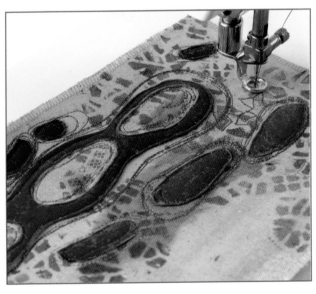

Create mosaic patterns using straight stitch and satin stitch on the machine. Small pieces of organza have been applied to this sample before stitching.

Here, shapes have been printed onto the background using a paper doily stencil and then stitched. Painted Evolon has been applied to represent balcony shapes of the Casa Batlló building in Barcelona.

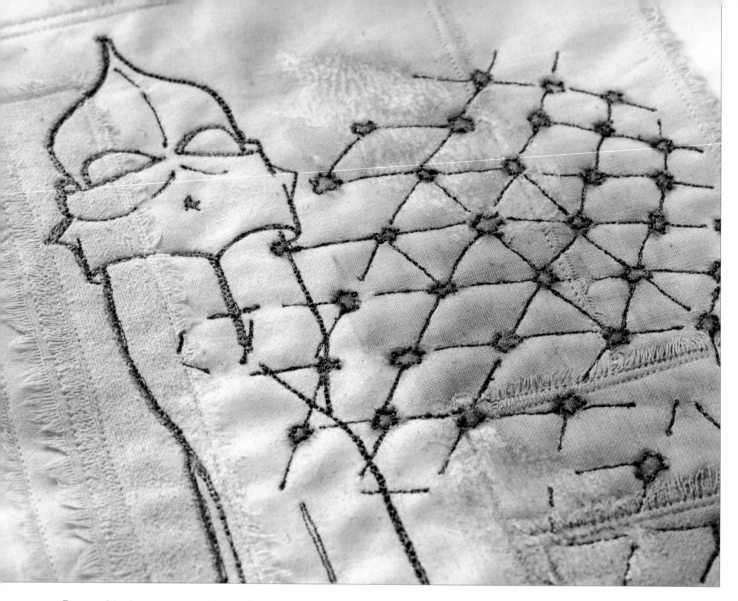

This part of the design was inspired by metal grids on windows in the Colònia Güell Crypt. The joints of the grid have been coloured with organza, representing the stained glass in the windows. The lacy pattern overlaps the strong shape of the stone chimney. The painted background shows the contrast between the silk noil and calico with the distressed effect of the horticultural fleece.

This section was inspired by the snake-like benches in Parc Güell. The curved shapes are covered in mosaics. I have used several colours to stencil through a paper doily, masking the area to control the application. Additional fabrics were then applied and machine stitched.

These shapes were taken from two of the mosaic, plant-inspired chimneys on the roof of the Palau Güell. Shapes have been outlined and highlighted, with additional stitch adding texture.

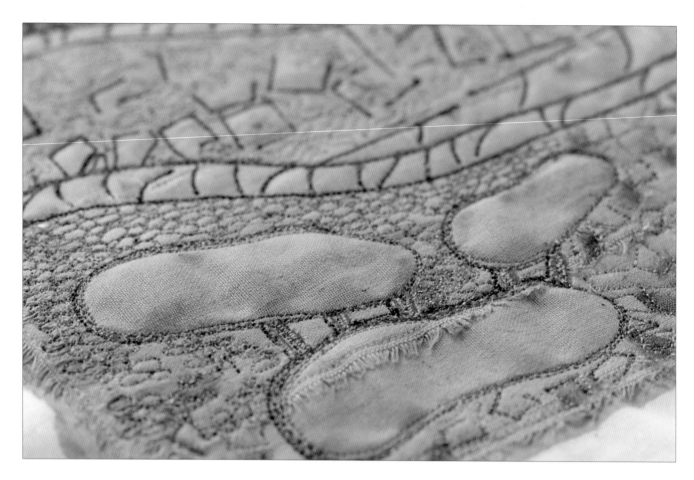

As you are working, leave some quiet, calm areas that will contrast against the more intricate detailed stitching.

The stitch direction on the snake-like ridges creates a three-dimensional illusion. In some areas, using a thread colour that matches the background gives a textural quality whilst allowing subtle blending of colours.

The contrast here is emphasised with the textured stitching on the receding chimney shape. Granite stitch provides surface interest but, again, I have kept the colours similar.

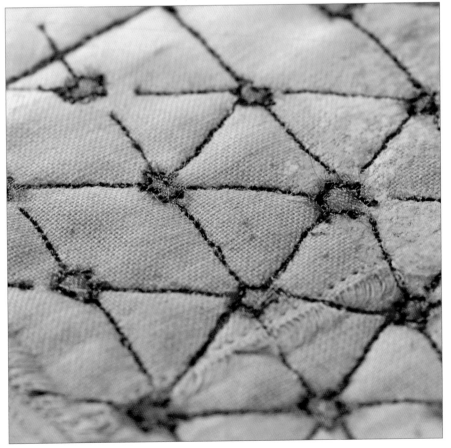

The organza fabric within the grid pattern gives a slight shimmer to the surface, catching the light.

Architecture gallery

Venetian Facade
46 x 70cm (18 x 27½in)

The city of Venice has been a great inspirational source for my artwork. In this piece I concentrated on portraying the contrasting textures of the crumbling, weathered brickwork and the elegant architecture of the windows and balconies. The limited colour palette I used evokes memories of the city for me. Layered fabrics were built up and rich surface texture was created by overlaying horticultural fleece, Xpandaprint and matt paint flakes. The mottled quality of the water was created by fusing horticultural fleece to the background. After painting, the surface was stitched.

Kilpeck Church
54 x 70cm (21¼ x 27½in)

Kilpeck church in Herefordshire is a stunning Norman village church and hosts the most elaborate carvings. My design was inspired by these decorations adorning the church door and medieval manuscripts, depicting the qualities of past times. Background texture was built up with layers of fabric, scrim and tissue paper with script transfer printed on to fabric. The surface was coloured with fabric paint and machine stitched.

Brighton 'On the Map'

41 x 65cm (16 x 25¹/₂in)

*In my current series of work –
A Sense of Place – I explore the
landscape, incorporating maps and
architecture into my layered and
stitched textiles. Every map tells a
story and invites the viewer to discover
new lands, visit new places and
remember holidays. I incorporate
iconic buildings and landmarks. This
piece combines the architectural
detail of the Royal Pavilion in Brighton,
Sussex with a map of the city. The
stitching emphasises the textures of
the landscape and the sea.*

Church Window, Brighton
35 x 45cm (13½ x 17¾in)

This work depicts the west window at All Saints Church in Patcham, Sussex. Torn layers of calico form the main structure of the piece and Xpandaprint was used to help portray the beautifully weathered flint walls. These contrast with the smooth stone slabs surrounding the window. I chose a blue and grey colour scheme to highlight the coolness of the flint.

Window
14 x 22cm (5½ x 8½in)

You do not always have to use paint to create a coloured, textured foundation for your work. This piece of work used coloured fabrics in a similar way. I selected fabrics with a monochromatic colour scheme – shades of blue – and pieced and layered strips to produce a unified design for this church-window background. Details were added with straight stitch, satin stitch and cable stitch, introducing a terracotta colour for a complementary contrast.

Landscapes
Rugged Moors

The rugged limestone landscape of the Yorkshire Moors is an excellent design source. With windswept trees and rough, jagged rocks, there is plenty to inspire artists working with textiles. This spectacular scenery boasts incredible views at all times of day but particularly when the sun sets, casting shadows and outlining silhouettes of trees. This project explores the use of texture to capture this wonderful landscape. An assortment of fabrics including scrim, silk noil, cotton batting and crepe bandage are combined to build up a rich surface, and three-dimensional crusty textures are created using Xpandaprint or puff paint. When the background is painted, the richness of the surface becomes apparent and the addition of coloured stitching, including whip stitch and cable stitch, emphasises the tree and details.

WHAT YOU NEED

GENERAL EQUIPMENT:

Sewing machine with darning foot or quilting foot

Embroidery scissors

Hand embroidery needle

Pins

Wooden skewer

Iron and ironing surface

Hair dryer

Baking parchment

Hot-air tool

Fabric paints: extender base, dark brown and terracotta (mixed with yellow, red and black)

Xpandaprint or puff paint

Brushes, sponge and palette knife

Tracing paper, pencil and marker pen

Coloured papers

Glue stick

Masking tape

Card

GENERAL MATERIAL:

Pre-washed calico

Selection of natural pre-washed textured fabrics such as silk noil, cotton batting, cotton crepe bandage, cotton scrim and linen

Tearaway stabiliser

White or cream cotton thread or yarn for hand and cable stitching

White or cream cotton machine thread

Coloured cotton perlé or similar yarn for cable stitch

Coloured machine embroidery threads

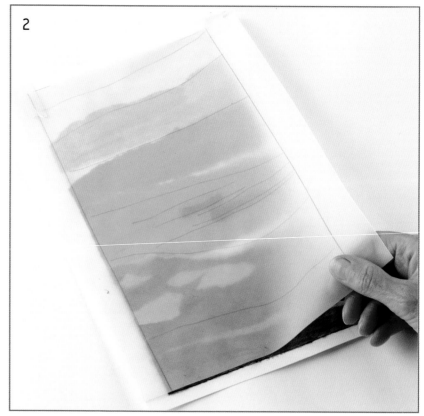

1 Plan your design and make a torn-paper collage to determine your colour scheme (see page 52). The papers help to represent the layers and textures within the landscape.

2 Copy the elements of your design onto tracing paper.

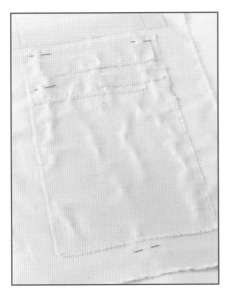

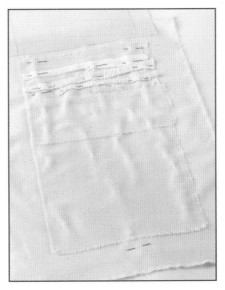

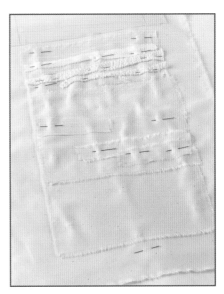

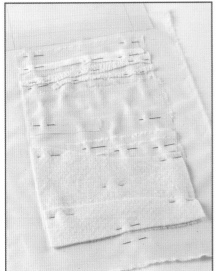

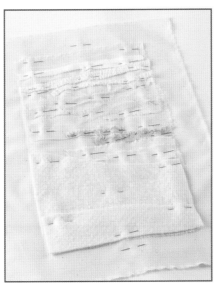

3 Take a piece of calico slightly larger than your traced design and centre it on a larger piece of calico for the backing. Select fabrics with different textures, tearing them into strips before arranging them onto the calico. Start at the top and gradually overlay each section until you cover the area. Heavier weight fabrics are more suited to the foreground. Lay your tracing on top as a guide to position the different layers. I have used calico, silk noil, cotton batting, white cotton, linen, scrim and crepe bandage. Pin in place.

4 Pin a piece of tearaway stabiliser to the back of your design and stitch the layers in place with white or cream cotton thread. For the rocky foreground, I am using a meandering straight stitch to create texture on cotton batting. As the layers are quite thick I am using a freehand quilting foot on my machine, but a darning foot can be used.

5 Additional texture can be added with hand stitching using natural yarns. Here I am applying a scattering of seeding stitches. Use a sharp chenille needle for this.

6 Work into your landscape with further stitching. Free running stitch, both by machine and hand, emphasises the contours of the design. This can be worked across all the layers, as shown.

7 To replicate the rugged surface of the rocks, sponge Xpandaprint or puff paint on to areas of the cotton batting and heat with a hot-air tool. Be patient, as it may take a while for the crusty surface to appear.

8 Apply masking tape to the edges of your work in preparation for painting. Mix your paint and apply to the background using a palette knife or brush. Merge the colours as you work, blending them together.

9 Continue to work paint into the different coloured layers, using your paper collage as a guide. Your fabrics and threads will all absorb the paint.

10 A paintbrush is best for colouring edges that need definition and for filling in any gaps. Try not to apply too many layers of paint as the colour will intensify and you may only need to dampen the brush with water to spread some of the colour around.

11 The Xpandaprint or puff paint applied in step 7 will resist some of the paint when you scrape it across the surface, leaving an uneven and craggy effect. The seeding stitches also provide an attractive contrast.

12 Where one colour in the design meets another you may not want the colours to bleed and merge. This can be prevented by using a piece of card as a block. Hold it under the edge of the fabric and work paint along it with a brush.

13 The abstract landscape background is now ready for surface stitching. Remove the masking tape and heat with a hair dryer or hot-air tool to fix the colour.

14 The windswept tree could be stitched freehand, directly onto the front of the design. However, you may prefer to transfer the outline shape from the reverse using tearaway stabiliser. Simplify the image while copying it onto tracing paper with a black marker. Turn the tracing over and copy onto a piece of tearaway stabiliser with a pencil.

15

15 To register your tree, position the tracing on the painted side and mark three or four points with pins. Identify these points on the reverse with a pencil or marker pen and line up the tearaway stabiliser copy (see page 53).

16 You can now stitch along the lines, making sure you have your chosen thread colour in the bobbin. Remember, it is this thread that will be visible on the right side. This process is just to transfer the main structure of the tree – details will be added later.

17 Now work on the right side and gradually build up the details of the tree using a straight stitch. Fill in the branches and trunk, adding delicate twigs as you progress, until you are satisfied with the overall design.

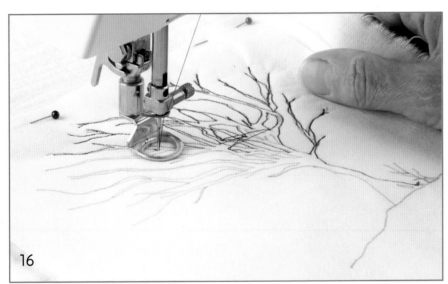

16

17

TIP
Keep your reference sketches, paintings or photographs beside you while you stitch to help you capture the growing shape of the tree authentically.

Wonderful crusty textures are accentuated in this detail. The combination of fabric, stitch, Xpandaprint and paint suggests the rugged terrain of the Yorkshire Moors.

The branches become finer and more delicate as they spread out to the tree's extremities. Looking through these branches you can see the detail of the landscape beyond.

Straight stitch lends itself perfectly to the portrayal of trees. The conscious use of stitch direction allows the branches to 'grow' from the trunk and flow to the outer edges, giving the rough effect of the bark.

Strips of cotton crepe bandage provide an excellent texture for landscapes. The raised, mossy effect contrasts beautifully with the smoother calico and rows of hand stitching. Cotton scrim also gives superb results.

Cotton batting produces a quilted appearance when sewn. The stitched lines sink into the surface, like rivers or tracks, leaving smooth, raised areas of fabric.

I do hope you have enjoyed creating some exciting textures in your project. The effects generated here could also be used to interpret moss, lichen or coral.

Poppy Field

Fields of poppies are a familiar sight across the countryside in midsummer, producing a vibrant sea of red. I have incorporated poppies in my designs for many years as they evoke different things to people. They are bright, joyful flowers as well as being symbols of remembrance.

For this project you will create a poppy field using layering and painting techniques. Torn fabric edges will suggest grass and coloured stitching will incorporate whip stitch using nylon thread. Chiffon fabrics are applied, adding texture to the swathes of poppies.

WHAT YOU NEED

GENERAL EQUIPMENT:

Sewing machine with
   darning foot

Embroidery scissors

Pins

Iron and ironing surface

Baking parchment

Fabric paints: extender base,
   Oxford blue, green (mixed
   with blue and yellow) and
   light brown

Brushes and palette knife

Wooden skewer

Masking tape

Card

GENERAL MATERIALS:

Pre-washed calico

Selection of natural pre-
   washed textured fabrics
   such as silk noil and white
   even-weave cotton

Tearaway stabiliser

Iron-on transfer adhesive

Red chiffon

White or cream cotton
   machine thread

Nylon invisible thread

Coloured machine
   embroidery threads

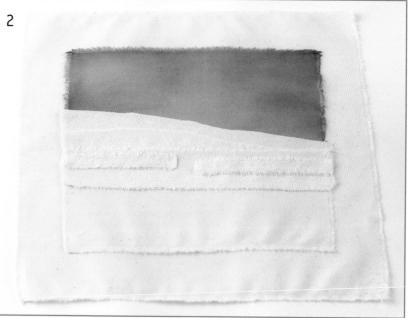

1 I have chosen to apply a painted fabric first for the sky in this landscape. Skies have a smooth appearance so I decided not to stitch into it. I am, therefore, using iron-on transfer adhesive to fuse the blue fabric directly onto the background calico. Paint a piece of fabric with your chosen colour. I have painted the sky with diluted paint, removing some of the colour with a paper towel to create a cloud effect. Cut a piece of transfer adhesive to size and iron it, rough adhesive side down, onto the reverse of the painted fabric. Use baking parchment to protect your ironing board and iron.

2 Peel off the paper backing, place right side up onto a piece of backing calico and iron in position. Now begin layering your natural fabrics. I have used calico as my base and then added torn strips of silk noil.

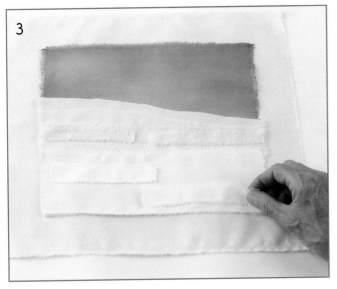

3 White even-weave cotton is my fabric choice for the foreground field of poppies. The torn edges will represent layers of grass. Pin in place.

4 Pin a piece of stabiliser behind, to strengthen the work, and machine stitch all your fabrics in place using white or cream cotton thread. Keep your stitching about 4mm (^{1}/$_8$in) away from the frayed edges.

5 Apply masking tape to the edges of your work in preparation for painting, then mix your paint to a thick consistency and start to apply colour onto your landscape. Along the horizon, use a piece of card to prevent the green paint spreading into the sky as you work along the edge with a brush.

6 Continue to apply the paint with a palette knife or brush, covering the distant hills. Hold the palette knife at an angle as you scrape the colour across the surface. Keep the colour paler towards the skyline.

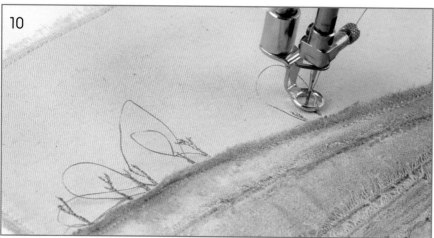

7 Work paint into any uncoloured spaces and under the frayed edges using a damp brush.

8 I am adding a light brown paint to the lower boundary of the fields, blending the colour as I work.

9 Carry on painting your design, varying the shades of green as you progress. Use a brush to blend and cover the surface until you are satisfied.

10 Along the South Downs you can see rows of trees on the horizon. Start to stitch a line of tree trunks with straight stitch. Don't make them too thick! As you move along, raise the presser-foot lever and pull through the top thread between each tree to make it easier to trim the ends.

11 Foliage can now be added to your trees using granite stitch. For this textural effect, run the machine fast and move the fabric in very small circles, filling in the area. It can be particularly effective if you set your machine on a very narrow zigzag. You can create interesting shading effects with whip stitch if you loosen the bobbin tension slightly and use two different threads (see page 27). Here I used a dark green thread on the top and a variegated green thread in the bobbin.

12 You can now continue stitching into the fields with coloured threads. Some variegated yarns can work well for this. Follow the contours of the image as you 'draw', adding texture and shading.

TIP

Layers of open zigzag worked across the design can give a grassy effect – turn your work 90° to achieve this.

13 To create the impression of swathes of poppies, apply strips of red chiffon to the surface, holding them in place with a wooden skewer as you stitch.

14 To achieve the effect of poppies speckled across the landscape, wind a red bobbin (soft rayon machine embroidery thread works best). Use a nylon invisible thread on the top of your machine and tighten the top tension. As you stitch, the tight nylon will pull up small loops of red bobbin thread. Vary the stitch length to create small dots or denser rows of poppies.

15 In the foreground the flowers are viewed in more detail (see page 126 for a closer view). Work some foliage and grasses and then use granite stitch to create small clusters of poppies. White daisies are worked with whip stitch. Keep layering poppies, daisies and foliage until you are satisfied with the balance of your composition.

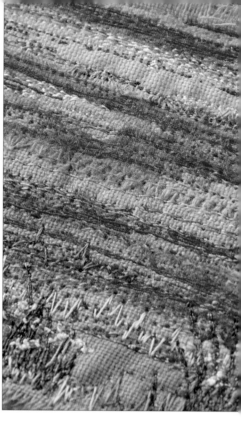

Strips of chiffon give beautifully soft bands of colour. Whip stitch has been used to create small dots of red as well as continuous lines.

Rows of zigzag have been worked across the fabric, providing contrast to the rows of straight stitching. You can see how textural the surface becomes when you combine torn fabric edges and chiffon with straight stitch, zigzag and whip stitch.

Granite stitch using a narrow zigzag setting creates a perfect filling for the foliage of the trees. With a variegated thread in the bobbin and a plain one on top the leaves appear to catch the light.

The foreground flowers are viewed in clusters.
Straight stitch has been used for the poppies and
this contrasts with the white daisies, which have
been worked in whip stitch. The combination of
colours softens and balances the composition.

The rows of dense whip stitch are raised from the surface like a cord and contrast with the smoother straight stitching. The frayed fabric edge provides a natural grass effect.

At the base of the trees I have 'sketched' with dark green thread to give the impression of shadows being cast by the sun. The landscape becomes paler in colour as it reaches the horizon.

129

Landscapes gallery

Summer Downs

12 x 16cm (4³/₄ x 6¹/₄in)

Cotton batting has been layered with calico, interfacing and silk noil to create the textured backdrop. Simple straight stitches worked by hand accentuate the contours of the Downs, as do rows of machine stitching and cable stitch. Horticultural fleece has been fused onto calico across the sky before painting, creating a subtle cloud effect. Cotton scrim was stitched in place under the trees, giving a background texture to the granite stitch, worked with a narrow zigzag setting. Xpandaprint and cable stitch give crusty layers for the rocks in the foreground.

Autumn Glow

69 x 51cm (27 x 20in)

This autumn-inspired landscape creates a soft, hazy atmospheric feel. Textured fabrics were layered with horticultural fleece, which resisted the paint to give a mottled surface. The trees and shrubs are less well defined than in Summer Downs. The paint was applied with a sponge in some areas for an impressionistic, misty effect.

Morning Glow

45 x 37cm (17³/₄ x 14¹/₂in)

Morning sunrise is interpreted in this landscape. As the sun emerges it exposes a glow of light represented with paint effects and subtle rows of whip stitch. The rugged terrain was created with layers of fabric, horticultural fleece, paint and stitch. Frayed edges were used to define the horizon and to add interest across the sky. By varying the length of the straight stitch, different types of tree have been formed. Whip stitch and granite stitch add to the foreground texture.

Three-dimensional inspiration

Creative stitched textiles can be transformed into striking three-dimensional objects. Fabrics can be manipulated, stitched, embellished, stiffened and formed in many ways, creating structures, containers and vessels, garments, body ornaments, bags, furnishings and book covers. Armatures, constructed from wire, cardboard or plastic tubing can be padded and covered with a variety of materials. Heavy-weight interfacing is an ideal product for assembling structures, boxes, containers and vessels. It can be painted and stitched, giving a rigid product for construction. Garments can be fashioned and embellished using different fabrics, from heavy-weight wools and cottons to fine silks and laces. Many of the techniques you have been introduced to in this book can be used to make cushion covers and other furnishings, as well as covers for notebooks and sketchbooks. Be imaginative and creative while you experiment with these ideas.

Wedding dress

It has always been a desire of mine to make and embroider my daughter's wedding outfit. My wish came true when I created her dress, designing and embroidering the lace that embellishes it. The bodice and capped sleeves are draped in the floral pattern, which extends and cascades down the skirt. Satin-covered buttons and a silk sash add to the detail.

Machine-embroidered lace

Freehand machine stitching was used to work the floral design on fine tulle netting. Water-soluble fabric was attached to the net, stabilising it while stitching. The stabiliser was then washed away, leaving the delicate lace. Pearls were hand stitched in position.

Embroidered lace, skirt detail

I enlarged the pattern and arranged it so that the design flows down the ballerina-length skirt. For the main structure, I used satin for the bodice and layers of net and lining for the underskirts. The entire dress was overlaid with the embroidered lace, which was hand stitched in place.

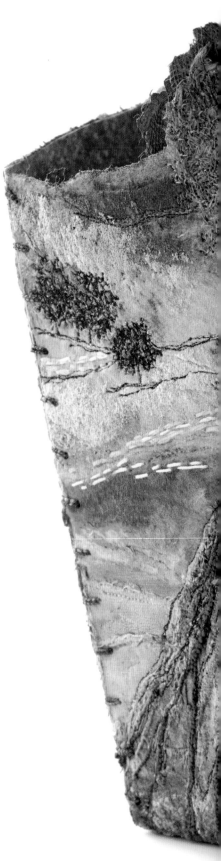

Changing Landscape

20 x 8 x 8cm (7³/₄ x 3¹/₄ x 3¹/₄in)

The constantly changing landscape is the inspiration for this vessel, constructed from heavy-weight interfacing. Each side represents an atmospheric moment in time. Fabrics have been pieced, layered, painted and stitched, building a sculptured surface. The stitches are functional, in that they hold the fabrics in place, and also decorative as they show line, form and texture. Xpandaprint and horticultural fleece add texture to the landscape and cable stitch gives extra depth to the piece. The surfaces are enhanced with machine and hand stitching, with machine-wrapped cords being used to represent tree roots and to lace the sides together.

Urban Landscape

33 x 20 x 5.5cm (13 x 7¾ x 2¼in)

Cityscapes provide interesting shapes and are ideal starting points for creating three-dimensional forms. For this design I explored the contrasts between the formal architectural fascias of the office tower blocks and the graffiti-painted walls, which can be seen throughout our cities. The structure is constructed with two layers of Decovil, a fusible non-woven interfacing. Tissue paper was screwed up and ironed onto the adhesive side of the Decovil, creating a textured surface. The design was worked into with freehand machine stitching before using a soldering iron to mark out the windows and to cut the shapes of the skyline. Painted iron-on transfer adhesive was applied to the graffiti walls with additional paint and stitch.

140

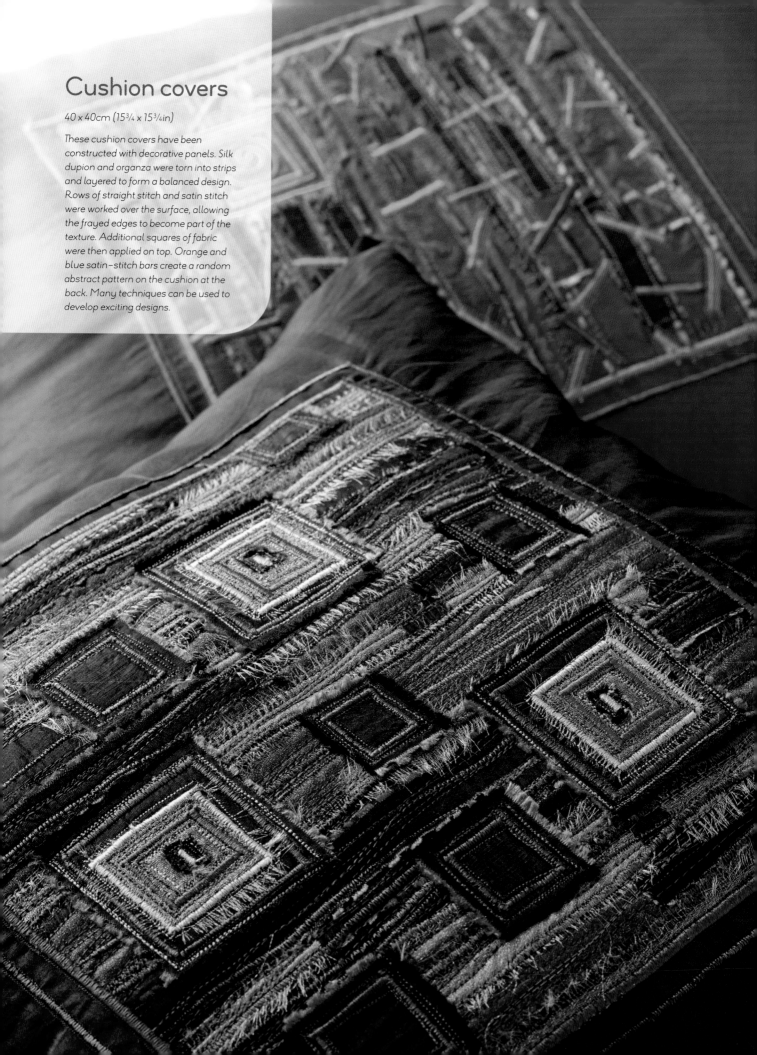

Cushion covers

40 x 40cm (15¾ x 15¾in)

These cushion covers have been constructed with decorative panels. Silk dupion and organza were torn into strips and layered to form a balanced design. Rows of straight stitch and satin stitch were worked over the surface, allowing the frayed edges to become part of the texture. Additional squares of fabric were then applied on top. Orange and blue satin-stitch bars create a random abstract pattern on the cushion at the back. Many techniques can be used to develop exciting designs.

Notebook covers

A variety of different sizes

A wide range of techniques can be used to decorate covers for notebooks and sketchbooks. Here, heavy-weight interfacing has been used as a base, covered with light-weight velvets. Strips of fabric were torn and stitched using a limited colour scheme. Imitation gold leaf and metallic thread add to the rich textured surface on the purple book cover, while cable stitch creates a crusty quality to a painted and stitched background. I hope that these examples will encourage you to experiment and develop your own fascinating effects.

Index

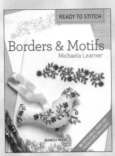
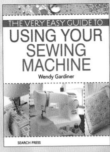

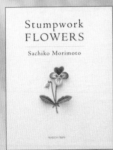

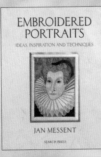

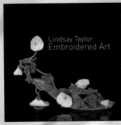

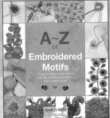